I0051182

Future Proof Sales Strategy

7 steps to rise above the chaos,
transform your team and take charge of your career

STEVEN NORMAN

"Steven Norman has written a highly valuable blueprint for de-risking sales and the go-to-market strategy for business-to-business selling. His insights are born from real-world experience gained over decades of sales leadership both in the trenches and at the highest levels.

Future Proof Sales Strategy is holistic and covers everything needed to succeed, today and tomorrow, in highly competitive markets. From understanding change in buyer behaviour to structuring your sales operation, hiring the right people, and then executing at a level above your competition; this book has everything you need. Other content includes how to a build a lead-generation machine, which tools are the best to use, how to progress and win opportunities, and defend and grow existing customers. Every sales professional and sales leader needs to read this book... highly recommended!"

Tony J. Hughes, #1 global sales blogger, best-selling author, top LinkedIn sales influencer and keynote speaker.

"Future Proof Sales Strategy is a brilliant summation of Steven's unparalleled experience, current themes from the world's brightest sales thought leaders, and critical trends that are profoundly shifting the sales landscape. Steven provides countless battle-tested strategies and techniques to help sales leaders absolutely maximise the output from their sales organisation in a more complex and challenging environment than ever before."

Jordan Mara, Modern Sales Expert & Founder, Coho Sales Consulting

"The future of buyer/seller interaction is truly shifting – balanced on a fulcrum of customer-centricity and trust. In this enjoyable and insightful book, Steven has clearly identified a framework for sellers that recognises that solving the customer's problem comes first, delivering on your promise comes next and the sale happens somewhere along the journey. It's the outcome, not the objective – but it's an outcome that Steven demonstrates clearly is good for both seller and buyer."

Donal Daly, Chairman of Altify, best-selling author of Digital Sales Transformation in a Customer First World.

"The world of enterprise sales has changed dramatically in the past decade with many sales leaders wondering where to focus and what direction to take. In this highly readable book, Steven Norman guides you through the key challenges facing sales teams today and then presents his seven steps for building a modern, world-class sales operation. Steven's deep, real-world experience at a senior sales level comes through in every page. Through this experience and his in-depth research he tells you what's working today and how to implement it. Anyone with a priority on building a competitive, resilient and dependable sales capability must read this book now!"

Brett Raphael, Managing Director, CrowdStrike ANZ

"The world of professional selling has shifted on its axis in recent years, with the balance of power tipping from sellers to buyers, never to return. Buyers are expecting more personalised, simplified and value-adding experiences from the vendors they engage with and voting with their wallets when those expectations aren't met. Future Proof Sales Strategy provides a step-by-step guide to understanding this new sales landscape, delivering practical strategies and techniques to help sales professionals and sales leaders not just survive, but thrive in this brave new world."

Cian McLoughlin, Author of #1 Amazon bestseller Rebirth of the Salesman

"When I started reading Steven Norman's book I thought I was in for another read on why we must all transform the way we sell. I have read so many on this topic recently. And sure enough, I got some of that up front. However, what was refreshing was that the bulk of the book outlined a step-by-step plan for how to transform – a plan that any executive could follow.

This is a perfect handbook for those wanting to drive change in their sales operation."

John Smibert, Founder, Sales Masterminds Asia Pacific

First published in 2019 by Steven Norman

© Steven Norman 2019

The moral rights of the author have been asserted

All rights reserved. Except as permitted under the *Australian Copyright Act 1968* (for example, a fair dealing for the purposes of study, research, criticism or review), no part of this book may be reproduced, stored in a retrieval system, communicated or transmitted in any form or by any means without prior written permission.

All enquiries should be made to the author.

Printed in Australia by McPherson's Printing

Cover design by Designerbility
Editing and book production by Grammar Factory

A catalogue record for this book is available from the National Library of Australia

Disclaimer

The material in this publication is of the nature of general comment only, and does not represent professional advice. It is not intended to provide specific guidance for particular circumstances and it should not be relied on as the basis for any decision to take action or not take action on any matter which it covers. Readers should obtain professional advice where appropriate, before making any such decision. To the maximum extent permitted by law, the author and publisher disclaim all responsibility and liability to any person, arising directly or indirectly from any person taking or not taking action based on the information in this publication.

Contents

Part 1: Understanding Today's Sales Landscape

Part 2: Seven Steps to a Next-Gen Sales Team

Introduction: Embracing Change

'It is not the strongest of the species that survives,
nor the most intelligent that survives.
It is the one that is the most adaptable to change.'

CHARLES DARWIN

Across all industries, the business landscape is changing.

Digital transformation and the global explosion of connectivity has changed the way business buyers choose to research, evaluate and purchase products and services. A growing proportion of products and solutions are reaching market maturity, which has resulted in the businesses delivering those products and solutions facing increased competition, higher buyer expectations and price pressures.

At the same time, business buyers are facing increased pressure to minimise risk and deliver fast ROI, resulting in the rise of the buying committee, where the decision-making group has ballooned from a single senior stakeholder to up to seventeen representatives from the buying business.

The end result? Buyers have more choice than ever before, more access to information than ever before, and increasingly stringent internal requirements when it comes to business purchasing decisions. And all of this has influenced how buyers want to buy.

Ultimately, the sales profession has moved from a buying process that was intertwined with our own sales processes to a buying journey that runs very independently of suppliers and the sales function. Buyers hold the power, and if vendor businesses don't meet their expectations, they will struggle to survive in the changing business landscape.

This has led to widespread concern across the sales profession, with a building chorus of alarming media articles and industry reports all pointing to some huge challenges. Some of the headlines include: *Are Salespeople Becoming Obsolete?* (Fortune), *One million B2B Sales Jobs Eliminated by 2020* (Forrester), *Death of a (B2B) Salesman* (Forbes), and *AI and the Threat to Salespeople* (Forbes).

Not only are current B2B sales methods being questioned – the very existence of the sales function is being discussed, and the B2B sales profession is under tremendous, unprecedented pressure.

But what can the average sales leader do? In a desperate bid to keep pace with the quarterly sales treadmill, we work long and painstaking hours. Our days are filled with back-to-back meetings, hectic travel schedules, urgent issues and a never-ending list of top-down requests.

Front and centre is the ever-present pressure to make the numbers. Regardless of the company you work for, there is huge intensity and focus on the current quarter's results, from the top all the way down. This can become all-consuming for sales leaders, who face constant demand to be involved in every major deal, follow up with their teams multiple times a day, and complete frequent forecast reviews.

There's also a long list of stakeholders to keep happy, including customers, business partners, alliances, agencies, consultants, regulators and government. Then, once we've survived the sales quarter, it all begins again. Our job is a constant recurring sprint to the finish line.

At the same time, the profession is facing immense challenges as the business landscape evolves, and there isn't a single solution B2B sales leaders can turn to. On the contrary, it's becoming increasingly difficult for us to sort through the huge volume of sales advice available, and know which advice to follow and implement.

So what's the solution? How can the savvy sales leader boost team performance, stay on top of daily business pressures and not only survive, but *thrive* amidst the changes occurring in the B2B sales landscape?

It starts with understanding the challenges facing modern sales professionals.

The 5 challenges facing B2B sales professionals

The sales landscape continues to shift and evolve at an ever-increasing pace. In fact, with growing media coverage and social media noise, it can feel like the entire sales profession is on a foundation of quicksand.

After sifting through the noise, however, I've consolidated these changes into five major challenges B2B sales leaders, teams and individuals must face.

1. A savvier, more knowledgeable buyer

Where vendor salespeople used to hold the power in the B2B sales process (and received the incentives and commissions to match), modern buyers are savvier, more knowledgeable and more powerful than ever.

Buyers have wholeheartedly embraced the digital world, which has totally transformed the buying processes. As recently as ten to twenty years ago, buyers relied on the knowledge and expertise of salespeople to find the right solutions for their business challenges. Sellers engaged directly with buyers, qualified opportunities, presented proposals, and helped buyers make purchasing decisions. Today, with the rise of online reviews, video product guides and tutorials, FAQs and eCommerce platforms, the majority of buyers complete the bulk of their buying journey before ever contacting a salesperson.

In fact, according to SiriusDecisions, sixty-seven per cent of the buyer's journey is now done digitally, while CEB says fifty-seven per cent of the buying process is completed before the customer even engages with a sales representative. When they do engage, it's often only to process their order.

59%
COMPLETE

Customer due diligence
Customer's first meaningful contact with Supplier Seller
Customer purchase decision

Figure 1: Buyer journey, Source: CEB

2. An increasingly complex buying process

In addition to contending with a savvier, more knowledgeable buyer, the buying process has become more complex. This is largely due to the rise of the buying committee – a group within an organisation responsible for all major buying decisions.

According to CEB, an average of *seventeen* people are involved in every enterprise-level buying decision. This means sales representatives are rarely dealing with a single buyer, as even senior staff – including CEOs – have limits on their decision-making and buying authority.

Also, the buying is not always done centrally by, say, the IT or procurement team. Increasingly, other business divisions are buying products and services themselves. However, these functions are not necessarily familiar with B2B buying processes, which adds yet another layer of complexity.

3. Product commoditisation

Increased commoditisation of products and services is a fact of life. As products and markets become more mature, more competitors start offering similar solutions at competitive (if not cheaper) price points. Buyers become more educated regarding the options available while proprietary knowledge becomes more widespread. Many products and services are now sold on subscription models and what used to be complex IT purchases have become much simpler and easier to access with cloud-based offerings. This has made it easier than ever for business to try new solutions, and switch between solutions with low risk and relatively low involvement with their vendor.

All of this puts B2B suppliers in the difficult position of trying to maintain market share, and salespeople trying to hit quota, when their buyers see their products as interchangeable.

Simply, companies are struggling to differentiate their products in an increasingly competitive and complex market. Products that were once distinguishable in terms of attributes (like uniqueness or brand) have become simple commodities in the eyes of the market or consumers.

Commoditisation is a massive reason why companies need to have a cutting-edge sales capability.

4. Significantly higher CX expectations

According to a Walker study, by 2020 customer experience (CX) will overtake price and product as the key brand differentiator, and eighty-six per cent of buyers will pay more for a better customer experience. Additionally, with more businesses focusing on delivering outstanding experiences to their customers – both in the B2C and the B2B space – buyers won't settle for anything less than a stellar experience. And they will judge their experience throughout the sales process as indicative of their likely experience once they become customers.

According to research conducted by Zendesk, sixty-two per cent of B2B buyers purchased more after a good customer service experience, while sixty-six per cent stopped buying after a bad customer service experience.

At the same time, Salesforce estimates that it is between six and seven times more expensive to acquire a new customer than to retain an existing one, meaning that delivering an outstanding experience should be at the forefront of every vendor business's strategy.

Ultimately, the CX delivered by a vendor significantly influences both acquisition and retention, and because buyer expectations are higher than ever before, the experience also needs to be better than ever before.

Salespeople can no longer rely on product information and competitive prices to make a sale. Customer service will potentially make or break the deal. As a sales leader, this is no longer something that can be handed over to the help desk or customer support team – it is a business-wide responsibility, and that includes sales.

5. The impact of technology on the sales function

As I've already touched on, technology is having a huge impact on the sales profession. Many roles related to selling lower value or commodity products have already been eliminated as customers get more comfortable buying online and companies divert more resources to eCommerce platforms. The use of AI, chatbots and other technologies are helping consumers to make routine purchases just as or more efficiently as they would have with salespeople.

From a business perspective, replacing the sales function with technology has a significant impact on the bottom line, which means many vendor businesses are looking for any opportunity to replace the sales function with technology, putting many salespeople, teams and leaders in a precarious position.

The sales teams that will survive are those that effectively augment their processes with tech to increase their productivity and value exponentially. Those that don't just won't be competitive.

The challenge is using these tools effectively as, according to Marketo chief growth officer Jill Rowley, the proliferation of sales tech has the potential to hinder as well as help sales teams. 'If we go down this path and create even more silos of processes and databases within sales tech, we will create even more disparate systems, disconnected processes, disjointed analytics, and overly narrow views of each customer,' she says.

What does this mean for sales teams?

The challenges facing the B2B sales profession have very serious, very real consequences – for salespeople, sales leaders, sales teams, and the sector as a whole.

1. Fewer B2B salespeople are making quota than ever before

According to a CSO Insights report, only fifty-three per cent of salespeople made their quota in 2017, compared to sixty-three per cent five years earlier. They liken it to running up the down escalator, where 'Buyers are getting better at buying faster than sellers are getting better at selling.' While many sales organisations are making incremental changes, buyers are exponentially changing how they buy.

Just consider these statistics:

- 67% of sales reps are missing quota – TAS Group

- 63% of salespeople are failing to meet quota – *Harvard Business Review*

- Only 50% of salespeople are meeting or exceeding quota – Aberdeen Group

67%
of salespeople are missing quota

If this were an isolated data point or a one-year blip, we would be right to question the data. But several data points have been gathered and reported over several years now, making it clear that the gap between the haves and have-nots is getting bigger.

Sales teams cannot incrementally improve their way out of this challenge. It's time to seriously consider today's sales approaches and be ready to make changes in how we sell, how we set up our organisations and how we manage our people.

2. Old sales strategies are producing diminishing returns

What worked even a year or two ago doesn't work any more, let alone persisting with sales strategies from ten, twenty or fifty-plus years ago, and the sales quota statistics quoted previously are just one measure demonstrating that this is the case.

So many of the tools, methods and approaches vendor sales teams are using are no longer effective, if not obsolete, and sales leaders need to evolve their teams to remain relevant.

The president of Covideo, Jason Price, shared his experience with prospecting efforts recently on *The B2B Revenue Leadership Show* podcast. 'One of the things that had really grown our business significantly, from about 2014 to 2016 and into 2017, was a straight-up call centre – an outbound cold call process,' he said. 'But the ROI on that activity really dwindled throughout 2017. So what we've had to do this year is incorporate a lot more email into that strategy, as a first touch, to really earn the right to make that call.'

This example highlights the constant need for sales teams to trial and implement new sales strategies, from prospecting through to customer success. Fortunately, this is exactly what this book will cover.

3. Sales no longer owns the customer relationship

As more functions have become involved in the customer's buying journey, and customer service becomes increasingly important to customers, the sales team is no longer the sole owner of the customer relationship.

We've seen the B2B marketing function take an increasingly impactful role and influence in the buyer journey, especially in the prospecting and lead-generation area. Where marketing used to have a limited role in B2B sales, the function now has excellent capabilities around targeting, content generation, activity tracking and measuring ROI. Subsequently, we have seen the rise of the CMO as a driving force in B2B businesses. We've also seen the rapid rise of the Customer Experience Officer or the Chief Customer Officer, who is tasked with overseeing customers' end-to-end experience with the organisation.

As a result, the role of many sales teams has narrowed to core selling functions, and sales teams that don't know how to collaborate with these relevant internal stakeholders will struggle to succeed.

4. Sales roles are being eliminated

According to Forrester, one million B2B sales roles will disappear by 2020, while Gartner predicts eighty-five per cent of B2B transactions will happen without salespeople by 2020.

Digitally driven B2B customers don't spend as much time with salespeople any more, while at the same time technology advances have improved our sales productivity. It's not surprising, then, that more and more organisations are scaling down their sales function, doing more with less, and ramping up in other areas like marketing and customer experience.

The final outcome? Sales leaders who don't adapt could get marginalised or severely sidelined, or will possibly be out of a job altogether.

What happens if these problems aren't solved?

Let's take two companies in the same industry, selling to the same type of customer. We'll call them Company A and Company B. Both companies operated under a traditional sales structure, with sales owning the end-to-end customer relationship. Before long, they were both suffering from declining sales.

Company A concluded that some of its salespeople were not up to the task and replaced part of its sales force. It also assessed that if its sales team worked harder and generated more activity, this would improve results, so it cracked the whip and drove more calls, more meetings and more pipeline initiatives across the team. It backed this up with additional sales incentives.

Unfortunately, these tactics didn't work. In fact, Company A started losing money, dropping twenty per cent in sales year on year. Within a couple of years, Company A had gone out of business. It happened quickly – and it was brutal.

Company B took a different approach. Instead of focusing only internally, it took notice of what was happening outside the company, with its customers and its target market. It realised that customers were buying differently – that they primarily researched online and didn't want to engage with sales until later in their buying process.

Company B also noticed that it didn't have good information about its customers, since these relationships were managed primarily by the sales team. As a result, customers were being managed inconsistently across the business. Without transparency and consistency, Company B didn't really know whether its customers were happy, whether they were using the products effectively, how likely they were to renew, and so on.

Company B recognised that it needed to be more customer-centric, rather than sales-centric. It set up teams who were expert at analysing the company's key customers and generating new leads. It implemented several CX initiatives to better manage customer interactions and ensure ongoing customer satisfaction. And it re-tooled its sales team to focus on middle-of-the-funnel activities.

Company B had a much better chance of being successful with modern buyers, and started generating record sales as a result. Company A – even with all the new expensive salespeople and a huge focus on increased activity – couldn't work out why it had failed.

The reason Company A failed to succeed is because it doubled-down on the old model. Its mindset was, 'Let's push everyone harder and replace the ones that aren't performing.' I see this a lot where a sales leader thinks everything's okay and that they're just having a temporary setback. They think that:

- While the world might have changed, sales is fundamentally the same.

- Results may have dropped, but it's not them – it's the market, or the product, or some team members.

- If they double-down on doing what they've always done, they will have a breakthrough.

- They prefer to push their teams harder, push for more results or offer more incentives, rather than make the big changes needed in the new environment.

- They might make some small changes but, as I said earlier, they believe that sales is fundamentally still the same.

- So many business and sales processes have been around for twenty, fifty or even 100 years. These habits are so ingrained that many don't even consider that we need to re-look at how we do things.

On an individual level, you don't want to be associated with that sort of demise. If you're the sales leader who resolutely sticks to the old way of doing things, your career will start to suffer. You could even lose your job.

Thankfully, there is a way to avoid all that.

Your guide to building a future-proof sales machine

If you are reading this, then you have already taken the first step to break out of the old cycle and create a sustained competitive advantage for your organisation and yourself.

This is your guide to building a future-proof, bulletproof sales machine – one you can point at a market with confidence, knowing it will generate revenue efficiently and profitably.

This book will help you:

- **Deliver more pipeline**. Not having enough pipeline is one of the biggest issues facing sales leaders today. I will show you how you can get yourself, your team and your company out of the negative pipeline spiral and start generating more than enough high-quality pipeline to exceed your targets, keep your team fresh and motivated, and avoid burnout.

- **Increase customer acquisition**. With the increased sophistication of buyers, going into new market segments or winning new accounts in existing sectors requires a new approach. Our approach to lead development and customer acquisition needs a very specific and specialised focus. I will share that with you in this book.

- **Improve close rates**. Declining closing rates are another threat, whether sales fail to close through continually getting pushed out or through losing the buyer to a 'no decision'. Some top sales thought leaders call 'no decision' our biggest competitor, and it is true – more deals are lost to 'no decision' than any single competitor you have. Implementing the structure laid out in this book should vastly improve the quality of your pipeline and therefore your close rates.

- **Improve customer retention and growth**. Customer retention and referral selling can be a tremendous growth engine for your business. Creating advocates for your products and company creates a virtuous circle. If we do our job right, once we are inside an account, we should leverage that strong incumbent position. We know acquiring new accounts and getting to new buyers is getting harder and harder, so we should look to leverage from our existing customers as much as possible. This book will give you a blueprint for achieving that.

- **Improve the quality of your team**. People are the key to sales success, and having the best people in the right roles – and with the right support – is the most critical predictor of our success. And we all know a high-quality team is much easier to manage. I'll share with you some breakthrough ideas on how to assess and select the best talent for your organisation.

- **Increase your team's performance**. If you are in a team with success rates of thirty per cent, forty per cent or fifty per cent, it can be demoralising. When teams are enjoying consistent success rates in the sixty to eighty per cent range, you can remain positive and view success as realistic and achievable even when you miss your target for a quarter.

- **Improve deal outcomes and profitability**. We all know salespeople or sales teams who are good at generating demand for our products but aren't able to meet our margin expectations. With buyers having so much information power and with increased commoditisation, we really need to change our approach and re-skill our teams to generate the value we expect. These skills are critical if we are to be valuable salespeople in the new environment we face.

- **Make yourself and your team hot commodities**. How do we secure our own careers and ongoing income in the face of these challenges and the 'great cull'? If you can adapt to this new world and become expert at driving change towards customer-centric sales models, then you will be more valuable to your company and your senior leadership than ever. I'll teach you how to drive the sales function forward and remain a strong voice at the leadership table, rather than becoming a victim.

Achieving these outcomes will require hard work, focus and determination. But a major sales transformation is much more manageable when it's broken down into smaller components and taken one step at a time. That's why the second half of this book is broken down into the following seven-step process:

Step 1: Implement the right sales structure

With so many changes occurring among B2B customers and how they buy their products, sales teams and company structures must change. This step will address the specialised functions, teams and structures you'll need to meet the challenge. We'll also take a look at the traditional sales structure and why it no longer works.

Step 2: Recruit and promote the right talent

Once we work out our structure, it is critical to put the right talent in the right spots. It is shocking how ineffective traditional hiring practices are in most companies. As we change our structure and start looking for different and more specialised skillsets, it becomes critical to develop robust processes for assessing our existing team and for managing the quality and fit of new talent. That's the focus of this step.

Step 3: Develop red-hot lead-generation capability

With lead generation and customer acquisition tougher than ever before, we can no longer sit back and leave it all to territory-based salespeople and sales managers. In this step, we look at how to create a dedicated prospecting and lead-gen function with key capabilities, including effective warm calling, account-based marketing, lead scoring and management, inside sales, and building a strong sales technology stack.

Step 4: Build high-converting MOFU capability

Building strong relationships just isn't enough any more – we need to bring much, much more to the table. Once a lead is generated, the focus is on moving a prospect from their current status quo to the business benefits that will be enabled by our offering. In this step, we'll cover techniques required to properly assess the current status quo (from the customer's perspective) and build the business case for change – qualifying and questioning, insight selling, storytelling, negotiation and deal management. We want our core sales team that manage this critical phase of the customer journey to be absolutely expert in these areas

Step 5: Leverage the customer experience and referral selling

Smart sales organisations not only recognise the expense of acquiring new customers, but also the potential returns of upselling and cross-selling to existing customers as well as generating referrals from those customers. With this in mind, these organisations are putting a big focus on turning customers into advocates and therefore generating strong referral leads.

In the past we would bring customers into *our* sales process and drive them through *our* funnel with a goal of closing the deal. We need to be going beyond this now with a customer-centric approach that isn't just about getting the sale – the focus must be on creating a customer advocate. That will then drive referrals and more business. That's what this step will show you – how to create a CX so positive that the customer does your referral selling for you.

Step 6: Invest in collaboration and stakeholder management

With multiple customer touchpoints, salespeople will need to work with other teams and leaders to get things done. The modern sales force no longer manages the whole customer relationship or all the customer touchpoints. Instead, these are split between sales, marketing and customer success. To be effective, we need to leverage and collaborate with those groups. In this step, I will outline a proven stakeholder management framework to boost collaboration and ensure success. We'll also discuss the importance of building trust with stakeholders, and how to do this.

Step 7: Focus on continuous change and improvement

Becoming proficient at driving and managing change effectively is a critical skill for sales leaders going forward. Poor or incomplete change management can really confuse an organisation, its people and its customers, leading to loss of business and key staff. In this step, I will share some methods and frameworks to help you prioritise continuous change and improvement.

A lifetime student of sales

My name is Steven Norman. I'm a seasoned frontline sales leader and general manager, dedicated to helping B2B sales leaders upgrade their knowledge and skills, build next-gen sales teams, and supercharge their careers.

Over my career I've been responsible for more than US$4 billion of sales. I've sold as a lone wolf and I've sold as part of a team. I've managed sales teams in consumer markets, small business markets and enterprise markets. I've sold direct to customers, and I've sold through channels and distribution. I've managed specialised acquisition teams as well as customer retention teams. I've successfully sold in Western markets and many Eastern markets. I've sold in developed markets and developing markets. I've sold products and services. I've sold hardware and software.

I've been through more than a hundred quarters as a sales professional and sales leader – many of them successful, but quite a few bad ones too. I've worked for some great leaders and had to endure my share of bad ones. I've worked for major tech companies, such as Dell and Targus, across the Asia Pacific region as well as small tech companies and start-ups.

I've always considered myself to be a student of sales and sales processes. This goes right back to the early days in my career, when I became determined to be the best sales professional I could be. I remember being made redundant in one of my first sales jobs. I was working in the computer sales division for NEC, the Japanese electronics company. I was doing well – winning multi-million dollar deals, making great commissions and going on president's club trips every year. Our products were manufactured in Japan and were very competitively priced, relative to their high quality, as the yen was quite weak for a few years.

This year-after-year success all came to a halt as the yen massively strengthened against the US dollar and the local currency, and we lost our competitive edge overnight. Ninety per cent of the sales force was cut, including my whole division, and I was out of a job.

It was a shock to go from being on top of the world to contemplating my future. I remember feeling sick at how exposed I was. As it turned out, I landed on my feet after a month or so, but this early shock made me determined to become an expert in the sales profession and make myself as valuable as possible to my employers and in the market. From that moment I dedicated myself to learning all that I could about the world of B2B sales – it has been a lifelong commitment.

These were the days of making first impressions count, asking open rather than closed questions, using qualifying techniques, addressing objections, and answering a question with another question. Ingraining strong sales habits, along with hard work, served me well and generated a lot of success at the time. But as I moved up, and as expectations rose, I realised I had to keep learning.

With this in mind, I immersed myself in all of the best practices around managing large customers, account planning, prospecting strategies, executive selling, negotiation skills and so on. My time at Dell, in particular, taught me the importance of constant change and improvement to maintain business growth.

At the start of 2017, I started Growth Acumen, where I work with sales and business leaders on implementing world-class sales best practices and developing their leadership. My clients range from large, multinational tech companies to fast-growing SaaS organisations plus a range of other businesses looking to scale up their sales capability.

It's up to us to turn things around

As you've probably gathered by now, I have been on an intense study mission of the B2B sales profession my whole working life. But in the last eighteen months, I've been able to dedicate considerable time to my research and analysis.

One of the things I've noticed is that, while there are lots of great, up-to-date books about specific aspects of sales and the sales process, a lot of them are directed at sales *people*. I struggled to find material aimed specifically at sales *leaders*, especially on how to equip sales organisations for the current challenges facing the B2B sales profession. This makes no sense, since sales leaders are the ones charged with the task of turning things around – and fast.

From my vantage point, I can see that many individuals and organisations in B2B sales are headed for extinction. They are facing a steady decline in their results, and by the time they realise their need to change it will be too late. Major customers will be out the door, key talent will have moved on, profits will have dried up, and options to turn things around will become very limited.

Don't let this happen to you!

Instead, be proactive and transform your sales team before the change is forced on you. If you do it well, you will gain a significant competitive advantage, with new accounts rolling in, existing customers buying more from you, talented staff wanting to join and stay with your team, and your own career advancing faster and further.

After all, sales leadership is about trying to impose order on something irregular and disorderly. To drive a process or a science over something that was historically human and artful. We have always been looking for ways to apply industrial principles to the sales process. That's what I aim to deliver in the pages that follow.

By reading this book, you're taking the first step to break out of the old sales cycle and create a sustained competitive advantage for your organisation, your team and yourself. Let's get started.

PART 1:

Understanding Today's Sales Landscape

5 Key Trends
Changing the Face of B2B Sales

'If the rate of change on the outside exceeds the rate of change on the inside, then the end is near.'

JACK WELCH

In the introduction, I touched on some of the major challenges facing the sales profession. Before we can focus on specific solutions to these challenges (as outlined in Part 2), it's important to fully understand the forces and trends shaping the B2B sales profession – including what's causing them and how they're affecting sales teams.

This is the focus of Part 1.

I want to be sure that we all fully appreciate the severity of the challenges we face. This is not a discussion of what might happen – these are very real changes already facing the sales profession, to the point where the majority of salespeople are not hitting quota, and Forrester estimates that twenty per cent of the B2B sales industry will be culled by 2020.

Change isn't optional. It is not a case of optimisation, best practice or making simple tweaks to improve already good performance. The B2B sales profession is in the midst of a complete upheaval, and change is essential for survival. And that change needs to happen *now.*

If you still aren't convinced, then just consider the five key challenges sales teams must contend with.

1 Responding to a savvier, more knowledgeable buyer

In the past, when a B2B buyer identified a need in their company that might require buying products or services, their predominant information source was the vendors who provided the product or solution you were looking for. Specifically, the vendor salespeople.

Any buyer looking for a solution was consequently subjected to an exchange with the vendor organisation where, in order to get information, they engage and give information about their company, their issues, their buying process, their budget and so forth.

As a result, for over a century – since the birth of modern selling – vendor salespeople have been trained to extract information about their prospects throughout the sales process, to pepper potential buyers with a hundred questions about their organisation, their priorities, their budgets, their decision-making process, their organisation structure and the list went on. From that point buyers couldn't avoid going into the vendor's system and being pushed through any associated follow-up activities and pressured to engage further.

For about 120 years, buyers had to play the vendor's game and abide by the vendor's rules. Since vendors had a near-monopoly on critical information, B2B sales organisations were virtually gatekeepers to the information their prospects needed and leveraged this position to their benefit. If the buyer wanted to seek out another information source, such as talking with other users for reference purposes, they would only be able to contact those users via the vendor and have to give up more information and power for the privilege.

In the traditional sales relationship, there was always more benefit for the seller and not much for the buyer in these interactions.

The sales process itself was linear: buyers engaged with sellers, opportunities were qualified, demonstrations and proofs of concept were done, proposals were presented and then decisions were made. Buyers and sellers were dependent on each other and the buying and selling processes were intertwined.

Buyer identifies need within the company

Buyer reaches out to salesperson from a popular vendor. Salesperson pitches their service offering

Salesperson ushers buyer through the rest of the purchasing process

Figure 2: Traditional B2B customer journey, Source: R2integrated

Today, the buyer journey has changed. Today, buyers explore digitally and can find out a huge amount about your products and services as well as competitors. The buyer moves between a range of sources – including vendor websites, search engines, social media and word of mouth – to gather nearly all the information they need before even speaking to an actual salesperson. They can also easily explore alternative ways to solve their business problem, all without engaging suppliers and salespeople directly. They embark on a customer journey, where they have much more control, much more independence and therefore much more power over the process and more negotiating power.

As a result, today's typical buyer journey looks something like this:

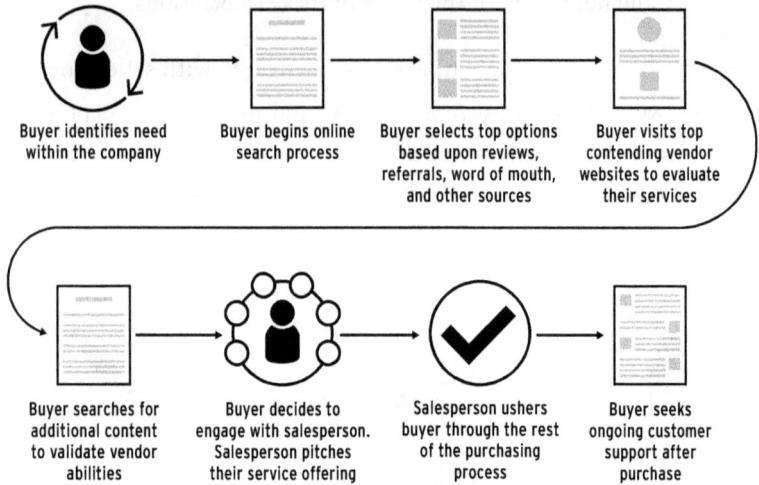

Buyer identifies need within the company	Buyer begins online search process	Buyer selects top options based upon reviews, referrals, word of mouth, and other sources	Buyer visits top contending vendor websites to evaluate their services

Buyer searches for additional content to validate vendor abilities	Buyer decides to engage with salesperson. Salesperson pitches their service offering	Salesperson ushers buyer through the rest of the purchasing process	Buyer seeks ongoing customer support after purchase

Figure 3: New B2B customer journey, Source: R2integrated

Yet, at the same time, most vendor sales teams are still running on the old model – assuming they are the guardians of all solution knowledge, and that buyers have to work with them to achieve their goals. It's no wonder that customers are largely dissatisfied and frustrated about their interactions with salespeople. According to the book *Insight Selling* from the RAIN Group, six out of ten meetings with salespeople are assessed by buyers as 'not valuable, or don't live up to expectations'.

As sales leaders, can we really be surprised that, when given the tools and the opportunity, buyers have embraced independent research?

Today, smart companies are investing heavily to understand the buyer journey for their specific customers and to ensure they are developing and mapping sales and marketing activities against this journey.

Of course this results in a lot of digital activities designed to catch potential customers early in their buying process and develop them towards becoming a lead.

Nowadays, buyers are much more likely to access – and be influenced by – reviews, referrals and other such sources. According to a survey conducted by Dimensional Research, two thirds of buyers read online reviews, and ninety per cent said positive online reviews influenced their buying decisions.

Ultimately, salespeople are no longer buyers' go-to source for information. According to Forrester, salespeople come fifth on the list of sources buyers use for research when looking for a new mobile device – after peers, analysts, IT forums and tech publications.

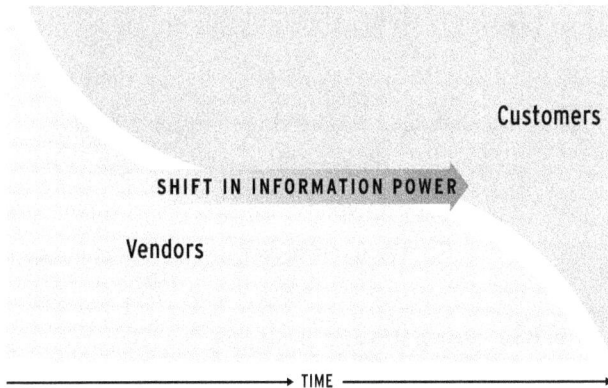

Figure 4: Information power shift

And this isn't just the case for simple, out-of-the-box solutions. The data shows that buyers are becoming increasingly comfortable buying more complex and expensive products and services without consulting, or at the least delaying their interaction, with salespeople. According to CEB, the average business buyer is fifty-seven per cent of their way through their buying journey before engaging with a salesperson. According to SiriusDecisions, sixty-seven per cent of a buyer's journey is done digitally, while Forrester found that *seventy-four per cent* of business buyers perform more than half of their research online before buying offline.

67% of the buyer's journey is done digitally

That's why – when we do actually get that slot with the customer – it's critical that we maximise that time as much as possible. Twenty years ago we were trained to ask customers what keeps them awake at night. We can't do that any more – not only is it going to chew up valuable customer-facing time, but we should already have some idea of what their major concerns and challenges are. We need to go into that meeting fully prepared to bring value.

B2B companies tend to be more conservative than their B2C counterparts, in the sense that they can be slower to react to this change in buyer behaviour. Also, if you recall the CSO Insights data on sales performance, the decline in overall B2B sales performance has been gradual. Perhaps we've noticed our performance is dropping a bit year after year, but it's not dramatic – it has happened gradually. This has caught many B2B sales professionals off guard.

However, many companies are now attempting to restore the balance of power between buyer and seller by leveraging emerging technologies, processes and organisational structures (which we'll discuss in Part 2).

Rather than merely reacting to the journeys that consumers themselves devise, companies are shaping their paths, leading rather than following.

Marketers, in particular, are increasingly managing journeys as they would any product. As a result, journeys are becoming central to the customer's experience of a brand – and as important as the products or services themselves in providing competitive advantage.

2 The rise of the buying committee

Every year CEB surveys how many people are involved in business buying decisions, and for the past few years the numbers have been going up. In 2014 they calculated that there were an average of 5.4 people involved in business buying decisions, while in 2017 that number had climbed to 6.8. They also found that in large enterprise decisions there were an average of *seventeen* people involved.

I had a discussion with Michele Buckley, global sales and marketing adviser at Gartner, which backed up these findings. 'Buying is being done by larger teams than ever before,' says Michele. 'A lot of sales reps say, "I just need to get to the senior decision maker and then everything will flow smoothly." This is fool's gold – it doesn't exist. There is no longer a single decision maker – this is just some of the conventional sales wisdom that no longer applies in today's sales world.

'Our research is showing that, to make a technology purchase, there is a core team of eight people, with **17** is the average number of people involved in an enterprise-buying decision another five to six people who just pop in and out occasionally. I like to think of them as seagulls. They kind of just fly into a meeting, poop on your proposal and then fly out again – and perhaps toss in some kind of security or compliance requirement that the buying team didn't anticipate and needs to adapt to.

'In addition, we're finding that this buying team could be led by IT. It could be led by business. It could be led by a cross-functional team, or a senior executive. That leadership will be different, company to company. It can also differ during the life of the purchase process. It might start with one particular leader, but that changes to a different leader at the end. So, it's actually incredibly dynamic – you might even say chaotic.

'When you think about having fourteen people in a room trying to make a decision, it takes longer to generate consensus. Building that consensus is very time-consuming. The number of communications that are required is also time-consuming.

'There are some other factors making the sales cycles longer. One of them is that there are multiple approvals that need to be sought. Cost and risk consistently come up as key objections. In fact, we're finding that fifty per cent of buyers are running into costs as an objection and fifty-three per cent are running into risk as an objection.

'These objections take quite a long time to resolve. Our clients are telling us it takes anywhere between two and three months just to resolve any objections raised around cost and risk. Risk is one of those areas that a lot of sellers don't think to address throughout the sales cycle. Therefore, it leads to further delays.'

As the buying process becomes longer and more complicated, sellers must find ways to help buyers navigate the process.

HELPING BUYERS NAVIGATE THE BUYING PROCESS

As sellers, we might be forgiven for thinking the role of the buyer is easy. In fact, being a buyer in an increasingly complex enterprise world is actually quite difficult, because the buyer has to have a real understanding of the problems they face, and how those problems affect all the relevant stakeholders within the business. Then, they have to navigate potential solutions in the market.

'A well-informed seller should actually be able to guide that conversation,' says Donal Daly, Chairman of Altify, and one of the most prominent thought leaders in the sales world.

'They should be able to help the seller get a better understanding of the problem they have, get a better understanding of potential solutions, and get a better understanding of other issues that might be impacted by the solution they're thinking of implementing.'

As the buying process continues to get more complex, Donal says it becomes increasingly important to understand *how* the buyer wants to buy.

'I break it down into three models, based on three different types of customers – the customer who says, "Help me buy", the customer who says, "Guide me" and the customer who says, "Partner with me." So, across those three different lanes of the customer journey, what the sales engagement model needs to look like is different,' he says.

Here's an overview of each customer, along with some guidelines on how best to engage them.

Help me buy

This customer generally knows what they want to buy, and the impact of their purchase on their organisation. They don't necessarily want to develop a long-term strategic relationship with the salesperson. They'll simply say,

'Make sure that what you have meets my needs, and help me buy it.'

If the customer says, 'Help me buy', then we probably don't want to invest the time to be a trusted adviser. We probably want to have technology that helps bring them through the funnel. This means making sure that, in the earlier stages, we're dealing with the customer's requirements, and understanding how they buy.

This means asking a series of questions like, 'What does procurement need to do? What does legal need to do? What are your tech specs?' Those kinds of things. It's about understanding the customer's buying process.

The technology to be applied in that case is a guided selling process, which makes sure that the seller doesn't miss out any of the customer's buying process steps, fundamentally. They don't need to do a ton of discovery, in the classic sense, because the buyer says, 'Here are ten things that I need.'

Guide me

Again, this customer generally knows what they want. At the very least, they know what issues they're having. So, they want the salesperson to guide them towards anything they haven't thought of yet, and then help them come up with a solution.

When we get into this second lane of the customer journey, it gets a bit more complex. The customer is saying, 'I want to buy something', but here we get into questions like, 'Who are all the stakeholders? Are there business problems that we're actually trying to solve?'

As we step into that, the technology that needs to be applied is, hopefully, AI-powered, which points out weaknesses in the buyer-seller relationship, misalignment of the customer's business problem and how we're solving it, and so on.

Partner with me

This is where the customer says, 'I have a vision, but I haven't worked out the logistics; I don't know how I'm going to get there. I want you to be my partner long term.'

This is where we need to bring together all the resources of the company to achieve that long-term vision for the customer. At this stage, we need some kind of collaborative, account-based approach.

So, different technology pieces apply, and different sales engagement models apply. But it all starts with how the customer wants to interact.

We'll go into some detail on how to navigate through the increasingly complex buying process later, but suffice to say for now that it requires careful planning, precise execution and a huge amount of effort. We really need salespeople managing these 'middle-of-the-funnel' activities to be very professional and capable in manoeuvring effectively through the buying process.

3 Combating product commoditisation

Victor Antonio, a keynote conference speaker on sales motivation, refers to product commoditisation as 'the equality of quality'.

'By that, I mean that almost every product or every service is the same. That's the equality of quality,' he says.

In any given product category, the options available are all of a similar quality and deliver a similar benefit. This means they are much more interchangeable. The rise of subscription models, in particular, offers buyers a low-risk option to sign up to a product or service online, and switch to something else if they don't like it.

A lot of product categories that used to be complex are now not so complex at all. Think about how difficult it used to be to buy and install computer systems, software programs and other technical products. There were a lot of considerations around installation, training, maintenance and other factors. It involved hours of discussions, meetings and proposals, and the involvement of a team of engineers and other specialists.

This was obviously good for sellers, as solutions could not be easily compared, and there was a degree of complexity that involved the customer deeply engaging with the supplier. Now customers buy mobile phones, personal computers and other technology products with a few clicks on a website.

Suppliers have been adapting or springing up to meet the consumer-like expectations of business buyers. Even software solutions that used to be extremely complex to customise and implement can be very straightforward to buy and use quickly. Take, for example, Xero, the cloud-based accounting solution. You can sign up online and start using it straightaway. Compare this to installing a new accounting system a decade ago. It could be an enormous and risky task, requiring a huge amount of evaluation, testing, planning and training.

These days, a lot of the software we use sits in the cloud. We use it as a service, without any consideration of, 'Is that going to work well with Windows? Or Mac?' Compatibility's not an issue. This has lowered the barriers for customers to access different products and solutions, and for the various business units within companies to buy a lot more. Before, if you wanted to buy software, you'd have to go through the IT department, which was an almost impossible task because of the rigmarole of evaluation and testing required.

Today, if a marketing manager wanted to try a new marketing automation tool from an overseas vendor, they could sign up to a subscription for twenty dollars a month and get access to a tool that will perform a niche function that they couldn't previously do in-house. They wouldn't need to fill out a proposal with procurement or put it through IT – it's as simple and straightforward as any B2C interaction.

At the same time, buyers want to keep their options open for as long as possible – with so many options available, they'd prefer not to tie themselves into a supplier or even a type of solution too early in the process. They want to be able to research and compare approaches, and have some internal discussion before getting engaged with vendors.

Let's consider, for example, that a potential customer is given a mission by the CFO to reduce IT expenses by ten per cent. Now think about all the potential ways to solve that problem – outsourcing all or part of the IT function, reducing IT service levels to the organisation, using creative financing to sell and lease back equipment, not supporting some legacy systems, reducing headcount, replacing older systems with newer cloud-based solutions, or changing the IT department from a cost centre to a profit centre that charges each business division based on service levels, to name just a few.

The person given this task will probably not want to start engaging in relationships with potential suppliers straightaway – they will want to research the potential approaches first and start digging into potential suppliers only once the solution has been narrowed down.

The main impact of product commoditisation is that your sales capability – rather than your product or service – is now the key differentiator. In other words, having a world-class sales team is more important than ever, as it is now the most powerful way to stand out in the market and resonate with buyers.

'Because everything looks the same, the key differentiator is the ability of the salesperson to guide the customer's behaviour and decision-making process,' says Victor.

'Far from being redundant, the salesperson is more important than ever in today's market. Because buyers have more information, it's got to the point where it's *too much* information. This is why I believe that the salesperson is now more valuable than ever.'

In order to combat product commoditisation, Victor believes we need to think of ourselves as advisers rather than sellers.

Products are commoditised, services are commoditised, but what can't be commoditised is the salesperson's ability to provide a unique solution

'First, it's crucial for the salesperson to understand their own business, the customer's business and the market environment. Then they can approach a potential customer as an adviser,' he says.

'Today's buyer is looking for clarity – they want us to tell them things they don't know. So, instead of launching straight into a product pitch, the salesperson might say, "Let me reduce the clutter and the noise for you. Here's what you're not seeing."

'Every customer is somewhere on a scale between certainty and anxiety. Sometimes, they have an equal amount of both. That means the sale is not going to happen. Or if they have too much anxiety, the sale is definitely not going to happen.

'But by offering the customer insights and clarification, and by telling them things they don't know, we can increase their certainty of what they're buying and reduce their anxiety. That's how we sell successfully in today's market.'

4   Meeting significantly higher CX expectations

Modern B2B buyers expect their enterprise-buying experiences to match the ease and comfort of their consumer-buying experiences. For example, customers accustomed to the personalisation and ease of dealing with companies like Google and Amazon now expect the same kind of service from all companies. And if they don't get it, they have no qualms about looking elsewhere.

Research from Thunderhead and Populus shows twenty-five per cent of customers will switch providers after just one negative customer experience. In short, B2B buyers expect B2B purchases to be as seamless and satisfactory as their B2C experiences.

We can respond to this by shifting some of our focus from lead generation to customer experience. Traditional B2B marketing strategies focused on generating quality leads, which sales teams could then push through the funnel. To generate these leads, marketing would 'gate' content like whitepapers, forcing users to fill out a contact form before they could access the document.

Nowadays, many of today's B2B buyers are too savvy to get sucked into the funnel via gated content. In fact, a LinkedIn report found eighty-seven per cent of buyers decided not to download content due to gating. Buyers know they can go elsewhere to find the information they're seeking. So, instead of 'hiding' information from potential buyers, we should share it openly. Far from doing ourselves a disservice, this can actually boost business. A DemandGen survey revealed eighty-seven per cent of buyers said the solution provider they chose provided ample content to help them through each stage of the decision-making process.

Improving post-sale customer experience is also important – and can also prove highly profitable. Since reviews, referrals and word of mouth are some of the strongest influencers on B2B buying decisions, post-sale customer satisfaction is key to creating future customer advocates.

According to the *Harvard Business Review*, eighty-four per cent of B2B buyers begin the purchasing process with a referral, while peer recommendations influence more than ninety per cent of all B2B buying decisions. With this in mind, it's more important than ever to perfect the post-sale experience, as it encourages customer loyalty and, in turn, can help us attract more customers.

This is one of the reasons why we've seen the rise of the Customer Experience Officer, or the Chief Customer Officer. These roles often have a broad brief way beyond the scope of the traditional customer service or technical support role. They are tasked with paying attention to, and improving, the complete end-to-end experience customers have with an organisation. They look at all of the touchpoints, from the time a customer first makes contact with the company and throughout the entire lifecycle.

Rather than focusing on individual interaction touchpoints, we need to focus on the entire customer journey, which spans a progression of touchpoints, and has a clearly defined beginning and end. There are two reasons for this. Firstly, even if teams execute well on individual touchpoint interactions, the overall experience can still disappoint, as evidenced here.

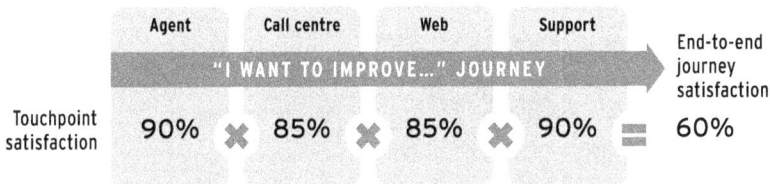

	Agent	Call centre	Web	Support	End-to-end journey satisfaction
"I WANT TO IMPROVE…" JOURNEY					
Touchpoint satisfaction	90% ✖	85% ✖	85% ✖	90% ═	60%

Figure 5: Touchpoint satisfaction, Source: McKinsey Digital Labs

More importantly, though, McKinsey research found that customer journeys have a significantly higher correlation with business outcomes than touchpoints do. According to a McKinsey survey, for example, customer satisfaction with health insurance is seventy-three per cent more likely when journeys work well than when only touchpoints do.

So why am I banging on about CX in a book for sales leaders? There are two key points I'd like you to take away from this:

1   It's critical that we prioritise customer success and CX, and keep it in mind throughout the sales process. We can't just be focused on closing the deal – we should have a clear goal of creating customer advocates who will become repeat and growing customers who generate gold-plated referrals that will further grow our business.

2 We need to recognise that our competitors are also doing their best to execute on CX and customer success and make it even harder for us to win over their customers. This is making the job of prospecting and generating leads in new accounts even harder and more costly.

To truly resonate with customers, we need to master the concept and execution of an exceptionally good customer experience. While this is certainly not an easy task, it is essential if we want to stand out in today's sales landscape, where the customer holds the most power.

5 Dealing with the impact of technology on the sales function

'The future of selling strongly involves technology,' says Tony Hughes, bestselling sales author and blogger, and founder of RSVPselling.

'Recently I heard that AI technology can more accurately detect melanoma cancer, from images, than a doctor can. Robots can do knee surgery better than a surgeon now. So, if these high-value professions are all at risk of losing their jobs, it's crazy to think that sales is going to be immune.'

Tech and sales guru Matthew King believes AI will replace ninety-five per cent of salespeople within twenty years.

'If I were an investor looking for a market to disrupt by automating a profession, sales looks like [an ideal] target,' he says.

That's not to say salespeople won't be considered valuable in the future. On the contrary, Tony believes salespeople will always be superior to technology in one crucial way.

'Where technology is powerful is in sifting through huge amounts of data, and in automating processes, whereas humans excel in creativity – in having empathy with other human beings and in building emotional connection. AI can maybe seek to imitate empathy, but it doesn't have the creativity and it can't really create emotional connection,' he says.

In order to survive and prosper in this increasingly tech-focused environment, Tony believes all sales teams will need to do two things.

'They need to focus on where there's huge complexity and risk for the buyer. Those human traits are going to always be necessary. Creativity and the human connection required to build consensus in the organisation, to get a business case across the line. Change management is a difficult thing within organisations, and the seller can help in that regard,' he says.

'Then, the other side of the coin is those sellers need to embrace technology fully. And they need to become excellent orchestrators of tools and platforms that can up their level of productivity. For example, there's technologies out there that can help you identify the insights that matter to buyers.

'The problem with technology today is most people feel paralysed by it. Every time they fire up their laptop, they feel like they're drinking from the fire hydrant. They're just completely overwhelmed with the amount of information.'

According to Nicolas De Kouchkovsky, an adviser and consultant to B2B software companies, there are now more than 830 vendors in the sales tech space – a fifteen per cent surge since 2017.

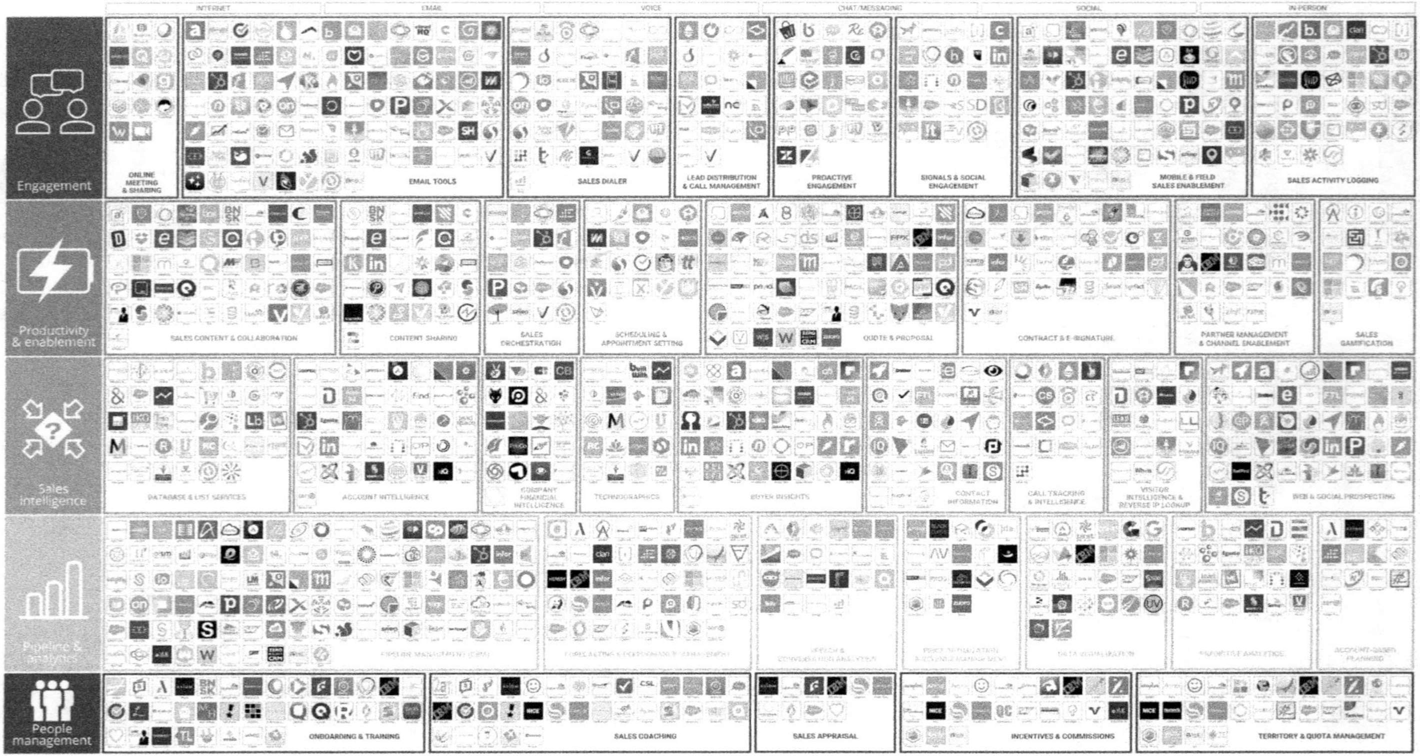

Figure 6: Sales technology landscape, Source: Sales Hacker

'The thirty-eight categories illustrate the extreme fragmentation of the market. Both sales and sales operations are sharing an increased frustration with the number of applications they have in their stack,' he says.

'The tools fragmentation ... can be explained by the specialisation of sales reps and the desire to get best of breed applications. However, it makes the workflow of sales reps challenging, sometimes offsetting the benefits of using technology. I'm hearing more complaints about the number of tools and applications to juggle.'

Nicolas says the plethora of applications is making the implementation of sales stacks much more challenging, because each solution comes with its own set of analytics.

'Many organisations are trying to log the sales activities into Salesforce or their CRM to consolidate reporting,' he says.

'... I'm a big believer in being able to visualise things to make sense of complexity ... I created a blueprint many years ago and kept on honing it to map players and apprehend new options.'

Figure 7: Sales Technology Blueprint

Interaction	Email	Voice	Chat/messaging	Internet	Social	In-person	Roles
Engagement	Online meeting & sharing	Email tools; Sales dialler	Lead distribution & call mgt	Proactive engagement	Signals & social engagement; Mobile & field sales enablement	Sales activity logging	Sales Representative
Productivity & enablement	Sales content & collaboration	Content sharing & consumption tracking; Multichannel sales orchestration	Scheduling & appointment setting	Quote & proposal	Contract & e-signature; Partner mgt & channel enablement	Gamification	
Sales intelligence	Database & list services	Account intelligence; Company financial intelligence	Technographic data	Buyer insights; Contact Information	Call tracking & intelligence	Web & social prospecting tools; Visitor Intelligence & reverse IP lookup	Sales Operations
Pipeline & analytics	Lead & opportunity management	Forecasting & performance management	Speech & conversation analytics	Price optimisation & revenue mgt; Data visualisation	Predictive analytics	Account-based planning	
People	Onboarding & training	Sales coaching		Sales appraisal	Incentives & commissions	Territory & quota management	Sales Manager

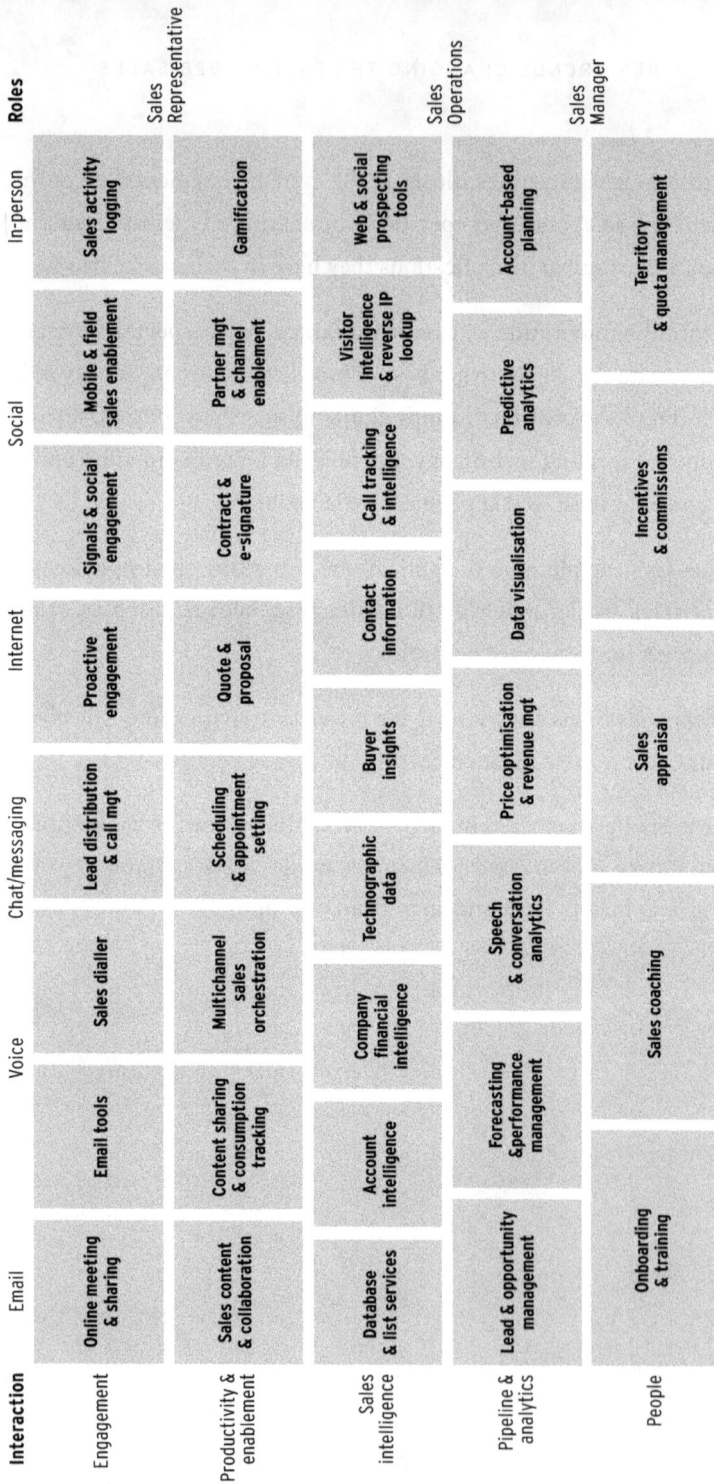

Figure 7: Sales Technology Blueprint, Source: Sales Hacker

Nicolas identifies three key ways to approach the sales technology landscape:

- Use the Sales Technology Blueprint to build a global view of your applications.

- Identify the functions that are foundational. Try to streamline these elements to simplify your reps' workflow and your pipeline instrumentation.

- Explore innovations and additions based on your sales process. Harness technology to either address remaining gaps or find new ways to optimise critical steps.

Make no mistake. The proliferation of sales tech will continue to have a major impact on the sales function. The most successful companies will not only capture the most data about prospects, but will also crunch that data and deliver it to inside sales reps in the right context.

We'll discuss this, and all the other solutions we've touched on in Part 1, in more detail in Part 2.

SUMMARY

That brings us to the end of Part 1. In Part 2, I'll reveal my seven-step framework for building a next-gen sales team. But first, here's a list of the key points to remember:

- Traditionally, the only way a customer could access information about a product or service was to engage with a salesperson. Now, the customer can gather nearly all the information they need before even speaking to an actual salesperson.

- Many companies are now attempting to restore the balance of power between buyer and seller by analysing and actively shaping the customer journey. As a result, journeys are becoming central to the customer experience – and as important as the products or services themselves in providing competitive advantage.

- Buying is being done by larger teams than ever before. Research shows it takes a core team of eight people, accompanied by another five to six in the background, to make a technology purchase. As the buying process becomes increasingly complex, sellers need to help buyers navigate this process.

- Thanks to product commoditisation, your sales capability – rather than your product or service – is now the key differentiator. In other words, having a world-class sales team is more important than ever, as it is now the most powerful way to stand out in the market and resonate with buyers.

- Modern B2B buyers have increasing expectations that their enterprise-buying experiences will match the ease and comfort of their consumer-buying experiences. The trend is clear that customers are putting a high priority on CX vs products or price when making major decisions.

- The sales function is being massively disrupted by technology. As well as customers being enabled to research and buy more effectively, the sales role itself is being re-shaped. Effective sellers of the future will augment their selling efforts by embracing technology. But with more than 830 vendors in the sales tech space it is no easy task to wade through all of the options and build the appropriate sales tech stack.

Seven Steps to a Next-Gen Sales Team

Now we move into the practical part of the book, where I show you how to build a future-proof, next-gen sales team. But before we get into it, there are a few points I'd like to make clear.

First and foremost, this seven-step guide is not absolute. It should be treated as a compass, or a starting point. There is no single or right way to structure a sales team, and there is no one or entirely right sales process that you should employ. Throughout Part 2, I include examples to help illustrate my points, but it's important to remember that every company and situation is different. Every company has different products, different channels, different industry dynamics, and so on.

I believe the insights and advice provided in Part 2 can apply to almost all B2B organisations. Whether you are selling to enterprise-level accounts, large corporates, SMB customers, or into the public sector, these steps will apply to you. There will just be differences in terms of scale and priority. For example, I am currently working with a fast-growing US-headquartered SaaS company. The company is progressively entering markets across the Asia Pacific region, including Australia, Singapore, India and Japan. They have a huge focus on getting new customers and establishing themselves in the market, so naturally there is a lot of effort on building out the company's prospecting and lead-gen capability, as well as its core sales function. While customer success and referrals are important, they are not a huge priority at this point.

By contrast, I have another client that is an established leader in its market, with around thirty per cent market share. However, the market is fairly stagnant, so this company is heavily focused on retaining customers and keeping them happy. It does this by leveraging its installed base to expand in current accounts and create customer advocates, and, as a result, generate referrals into new accounts. It is less focused on prospecting, since it already has relationships with almost every account in the market.

So, my advice in reading this book is to pick out one, two or three things that you regard as major priorities or challenges for your particular team or organisation. For example, if you face challenges with regard to lead generation, I encourage you to pay close attention to the step that discusses this. If you are having challenges converting leads into quality opportunities and profitable deals then focus on Step 4: 'Build High-Converting Middle-of-the-Funnel Capability'.

When it comes to implementing changes, I encourage you to start small – in one sales team, or one territory. Then, once you get the new practice working, you can replicate it on a larger scale.

But whatever you do, you absolutely *must* change. Sales teams should be like living, breathing organisms, which are constantly transforming and improving. That's why the final step in the seven-step framework is devoted entirely to change management and improvement. It will present you with a series of methods and proven tips to effectively initiate and implement change, thus ensuring the ongoing success of your career, your team and your organisation.

Let's begin.

Step 1: Implement the Right Sales Structure

*'No business can succeed in any great degree
without being properly organised.'*

JAMES CASH PENNEY

As discussed in Part 1, the sales landscape has changed dramatically in the past five to ten years.

Buyers have more access to information than ever before, with the ability to find product specifications, reviews, tutorials and more at the click of a button. They expect simple, seamless transactions where orders and payment can be processed without hassle, and any product easily integrates with their existing tools and technology. And they expect to have a stellar customer experience before, during and after the sale. At the same time, there are additional complexities in the modern buying process. Rather than a single stakeholder making a purchase decision, business buying decisions are made by a committee, with each member of the committee holding a unique agenda.

All of this leaves the traditional sales team in a difficult position. With buyers no longer reliant on salespeople for product and industry information, a lot of their value has diminished – at least in the eyes of the buyer. And when they do interact with buyers there are much higher expectations. According to Salesforce, eighty-three per cent of business buyers say it's absolutely critical or very important to interact with a salesperson who is focused on helping achieve their company's needs, not just making a quick sale. Seventy-nine per cent of business buyers say it's absolutely critical or very important to interact with someone who is not just a sales rep but a trusted adviser – one who can add value to their business.

If we want to resonate with buyers, we need to adopt a new sales model and structure, focused first and foremost on the customer. We also need to consider the best activities to meet the customer's needs, and how to organise ourselves in order to deliver those activities effectively. What is the best team structure going forward, and what skills do we need within our teams in order to reach and sell to the more informed, more empowered buyer?

In this chapter, we'll revisit the traditional sales structure, and discuss how it differs from the new customer-driven model. We'll also discuss some of the specialists you should consider hiring to sit within this new sales structure, and demonstrate the ideal sales organisation charts.

The death of the traditional sales-driven model

While the past century has seen dozens of sales methodologies developed and pitched to sales leaders as the ultimate solution to converting more prospects (just consider Relationship Selling, AIDA, SPIN Selling, Solution Selling, to name a few), the truth is that the fundamentals of sales have remained the same since James H Patterson established his modern, coordinated sales force after forming the National Cash Register Company in 1884.

Salesmen were trained extensively to develop an in-depth understanding of the product (cash registers), understand their prospects, structure sales conversations and handle objections. If you reflect on the various sales approaches that have been developed since then, you'll realise that not much has changed.

This is the traditional sales model.

In the traditional model, a sales leader would take their overall territory and divide it up into sub-territories, each with a sales manager or a branch manager. This division might be by geography or by industry, or by a combination of both.

Quotas were then set for each territory and rolled down to a salesperson level. The sales team and salespeople were then responsible for meeting that target and undertaking all the necessary sales-related activity in their territory to make it happen.

As the owner of their territory, the sales representative managed the end-to-end customer relationship and all aspects of the sales process. It was up to the sales team or individual salespeople how they went about prospecting, managing opportunities and servicing existing customers. Consequently, a large part of a salesperson's value to the company was this important link to customers and their ownership of the customer relationship. Outside the sales team, the company didn't have a good handle on customer satisfaction or future potential.

Marketing was in a limited, supporting role, providing the sales team with general market intelligence, competitive information and product information. The sales team then had to determine and curate what was most relevant to their customers. Sales would then manage the customer communication as each salesperson thought best.

Marketing also ran mass outbound campaigns to support sales and drive leads into the business. Usually these campaigns had a single message, rather than a tailored message for each buyer or type of buyer.

Messages were usually related to the features and benefits of the product, rather than the buyer's needs, and often revolved around a demand-generating offer.

The goals of the marketing team were somewhat separate from the goals of the sales team (making sales and hitting quota), making it difficult for marketing to know how effective their activities were and generate meaningful ROI data.

Finally, the customer service function ran very separately from sales and was focused solely on responding to customer issues. Customer service teams were measured on internal metrics such as response times, parts availability and cost management. External metrics – such as upselling, improving customer loyalty, customer retention and product utilisation – were less of a focus.

SALES owns relationship

Awareness

Interest

Evaluation

Decision

PURCHASE

SALES-DRIVEN PROCESS

Sales owns the entire customer engagement
Targeting and prospecting
Qualifying
Offering and proposals
Negotiation
Upsell and expansion
Escalation point for customer service
Inside sales supporting field sales

Marketing in supporting role
Sales support
Market intelligence
Collaterals / events
Marketing metrics
Mass outbound

Customer service a reactive function
Response rates
Cost management

Figure 8: Traditional sales-driven model

Sales as the ultimate goal

The traditional sales model had sales teams steering potential customers through a funnel, which was defined by us and our internal processes.

The focus was on contacting more prospects, getting more prospects into the funnel, doing more demonstrations, overcoming customer objections, and trying to close as many deals as possible by the end of each sales quarter. Phrases like 'Activity breeds results' and 'Sales is a numbers game' were common mantras, which came from a belief that we could control our destiny by driving more customer activity and deals through the funnel.

In short, the ultimate goal was getting a sale. Once the deal was done, the focus returned to closing more deals in the pipeline. The focus was always on making the monthly or quarterly sales targets, which meant all of our activity was determined by a never-ending quarterly treadmill. There was scant regard for the customer's buying plan. Instead, we would do whatever it took to shoehorn customers into *our* selling plan.

With the changes to the buying environment over the past five to ten years, this approach no longer resonates with customers and is producing diminishing returns. This is why it's time to shift to a new model.

Introducing the customer-driven sales model

The traditional sales model is in stark contrast to the new customer-driven sales model, which is designed around the customer's changed buying approach. Rather than individual salespeople owning the entire customer relationship, nowadays CEOs want their company to have independent control of the customer relationship with multiple touchpoints.

Sales will still have the lead, and an important role in managing the overall customer relationship, but we will be much better supported by the other functions within the business, namely the marketing and customer service teams.

Marketing plays a big role in the prospecting and lead-generation stage of the customer journey. The marketing team will identify key target accounts and develop detailed buyer profiles. They will design campaigns specifically for those accounts, customising the content and messaging to fit different buyer profiles. As a result, they will generate and develop leads, and track those leads until they are ready to pass to the core sales team (which oversees the middle-of-the-funnel sales activities identified earlier).

Meanwhile, customer experience will evolve from simply responding to customer issues. Instead, the focus will be customer success, and helping the customer get the most value from the solution they've purchased.

Finally, rather than sales owning the entire customer relationship, the relationship will be owned by the company as a whole. CEOs want independent control of the customer relationship with multiple touchpoints, rather than channelling all of their customer interactions through the sales team. Sales will still have the lead and an important role in managing the overall customer relationship, but will be much better supported by the other functions.

The implementation of company-wide customer experience initiatives has been a huge trend in the past ten years, so we as sales leaders need to recognise and adapt to it, and even leverage as much as we can for our own benefit. This is why the customer-driven sales model doesn't stop with the purchase of a product. In fact, there are four additional steps that come after the customer's first purchase – implementation, retention/satisfaction, expanding the relationship and creating customer advocates.

In today's high-performing companies, the sales goal is no longer just to sell something to the customer. Instead we should not rest until that customer is an active advocate for our products and solutions. So after we make that first sale, we should ensure the customer is satisfied with their purchase, is fully utilising our products, will purchase other products from us, and will continue to renew their contract.

Implementing this structure will empower sales teams to:

- Engage with customers early in the buying process
- Develop better qualified leads
- Have a stronger pipeline
- Improve close rates
- Generate better quality deal outcomes
- Develop a strong stream of referrals
- Leverage other functions in the business fully
- Motivate sales teams to accelerate their results

SPECIALISATION

Prospecting & Lead-Gen Function
Systemic & data-driven
Warm-calling strageties
Account-based marketing
Lead management & scoring
Mostly marketing & inside sales

Core Sales Function
Strong communication skills
Qualifying & questioning
Expert on insight selling
Strong negotiation skills
Strong leadership & teamwork
Foster relatioships based on value
Mix of inside & field sales

Customer Success Function
Grow product utilisation
Drive renewals
Business expansion
Partner with sales

ACCOUNT ACQUISITION PHASE

COMPANY owns relationship

REFERRALS

Awareness

Interest

Evaluation

Decision

FIRST PURCHASE

The goal is not winning customers / deals but creating advocates

Implementation

RETENTION & GROWTH PHASE

Retention/satisfaction

Expand Relationship

Advocacy/referrals

Figure 9: New customer-driven model, Source: Growth Acumen

The goal is developing customer advocates and referrals

Beyond increasing retention, happy customers will become a strong source of referrals. This is the ultimate goal of the customer-driven sales model.

Referral selling is a core component of the new sales approach. It should not be something left to the sales team as an afterthought, but rather an embedded and ingrained component of our sales and customer experience process.

With new business so hard to generate, and buyers becoming more elusive, referral selling is critical to our success. So we must start with the goal of creating advocates and generating referrals from them.

The power of specialised sales functions

I recently saw the CMO of a high-profile company present at an international marketing conference. I was surprised to hear him talk about the fact that his company was now embracing specialist sales roles.

The company had implemented a hunter/farmer model, whereby 'hunter' salespeople were responsible for finding and closing deals, while 'farmer' salespeople focus on retaining and growing business with existing accounts. The CMO said this 'breakthrough' strategy was the foundation of the company's B2B sales and marketing plans.

But this type of specialisation isn't new. In fact, it was first adopted by the insurance industry in the 1870s. Nowadays, however, there are so many touchpoints in the customer's buying journey that a standard hunter/farmer sales approach simply isn't going to cut it.

Instead, we need to build specialist functions and individual capabilities that will allow us to effectively and efficiently engage with the customer at each stage of the customer-driven sales model. Specifically, prospecting and lead generation; managing the core, middle-of-the-funnel sales activities; and creating customer advocates and boosting referral selling.

The days of the sales generalist are over. There is just too much expertise required in the various fields of customer engagement for one individual or one team to build expertise at a competitive level. Just consider the following:

- **Customers are actively avoiding salespeople**. The modern buyer journey sees customers using Google, visiting websites, sharing experiences and product recommendations in peer-level forums, studying analyst reports and reading expert product reviews. Vendor businesses therefore need specialised staff that understand where customers are searching for information. From here, they can build specific content and media strategies to get in front of these buyers.

- **Customers are harder to reach.** Buyers don't answer their phones, they don't return calls and they don't respond to cold emails. We therefore need sustained and expert effort to build relationships through various channels – social media, email, voicemail, text, phone and even old-fashioned snail mail! This lead development and nurturing is best done by a central team with specialised skills and the right data, tools and support at their fingertips.

- **The time spent with sales is decreasing.** Business customers are time poor, and want to avoid working with salespeople. If they need to, they want the interaction to be as quick as possible. As salespeople, we need to be sure that all contacts with the customer are extremely professional, efficient and valuable, and ensure the customer continues the process. Customers don't have time to talk about the weather or answer questions about what keeps them awake at night. Salespeople must deliver insight from the first discussion, negotiate effectively and close quickly.

- **More people are involved in purchase decisions.** The rise of the buying committee has made the middle-of-the-funnel buying process even more complex. Salespeople not only need to be experts in convincing the customer of the need for change and selling the benefits of the solution, they also need to help buyers navigate the buying process within their own company and achieve committee consensus. There's no way senior salespeople can effectively manage this process if they're also managing prospecting activity and customer retention issues.

- **Customer experience, renewal and referrals are critical to ongoing success.** There is a whole field of expertise focused on satisfying our customers in a proactive way. This goes beyond the traditional customer service function, which focused on reacting to customer issues. Customer experience (CX) and customer success is a proactive function staffed by experts in customer utilisation, product renewals, product expansion, referral generation and, of course, great customer service.

Ultimately, with the massive empowerment of customers in recent times, we need to be as professional and as skilled as possible in each of these crucial stages. A team of specialists is the only way to achieve this. By contrast, relying on the hunter/farmer model – or, worse, having a single salesperson manage every single stage of the sales process – is ineffective and will fail to resonate with customers.

With that in mind, here are some of the specialist roles you should consider for your organisation. Depending on the size of your business, the complexity of your products, and your customers, you may have more or less of these roles.

But regardless of your size, you need to consider how best to perform the key functions of lead generation and prospecting, middle-of-the-funnel sales activities, and customer support and success, even if it means combining two or more functions into a single role.

Market Response Representative

The Market Response Representative, or MRR, is tasked with following up leads from inbound marketing campaigns, including web marketing, advertising and other lead-generating activities.

They will qualify these leads and pass them on to either the Sales Development Representative (SDR) team or the Account Executive (AE) team, depending on what criteria the lead meets. The benefit of hiring a team of dedicated MRRs is that they help create a dependable stream of sales-ready leads for SDRs or AEs.

Companies often choose to hire dedicated MRRs based on the number of unique monthly marketing leads. According to RingDNA, a company should consider hiring its first dedicated MRR when there are between 300 and 400 unique marketing leads, although this number will vary depending on industry and customer base.

Sales Development Representative

The job of the SDR is to develop and nurture leads from your target prospect accounts. SDRs should be highly efficient in outbound activities – such as utilising social media, email, text, voicemail and phone calls – to generate interest in your products and services. They will leverage the latest technology and tools to track and score leads, and manage their activity.

They will be supported closely by the marketing team with market intelligence, buyer analysis and content relevant to each of the company's buyer targets. Once a lead is properly qualified (by meeting an agreed set of criteria), it will pass to the AE team to progress the deal.

Account Executive

The AE team will develop the qualified leads and turn them into customers. They will also maintain relationships with existing customers and look to further the company's business.

They are highly skilled at establishing credibility and building relationships with clients. They are also expert at helping customers identify problems that their product or solution can solve. They will then work with customers to help them through the buying process, negotiate mutually agreeable terms, and close the deal.

Account Manager and Customer Success Representative

These are two slightly different roles that manage the ongoing relationship with a customer once they have started buying from us.

The Account Manager is similar to an AE, but is responsible for taking care of *existing* customers. Namely, maintaining or expanding our business with them.

The Customer Success Representative is focused on making sure the customer is getting great value from the solution we have provided, and is highly satisfied, so that they will renew or expand the relationship. Once they identify a new opportunity with the customer, they will engage the AE to manage the sales process.

Most companies have either Account Managers or Customer Service Representatives, depending on the company's strategy, with a few having both.

Technical Sales Representative

Technical Sales Representatives (TSRs) might also be called Systems Engineers, Systems Consultants, Pre-Sales Engineers, Technical Consultants, Technical Experts, Technical BDMs or other similar terms. This team has the business knowledge and technical skills to help both sales teams and customers work out how the company's products and solutions meet the customer's requirements.

They will often design and recommend specific solutions, and be involved in explaining the solution to the customer. They may even develop peer-to-peer relationships with technical counterparts on the customer's side. They will usually be matched up to work with a group of MRRs, SDRs or AEs. The sales team will typically involve them in opportunities as soon as they need some additional technical support.

These roles will form a highly integrated team, with the MDR feeding leads to the AEs, the AEs delivering new customers to Account Managers and CSRs, and the entire process being supported by TSRs. Ultimately, each specialist does their part to ensure customer success.

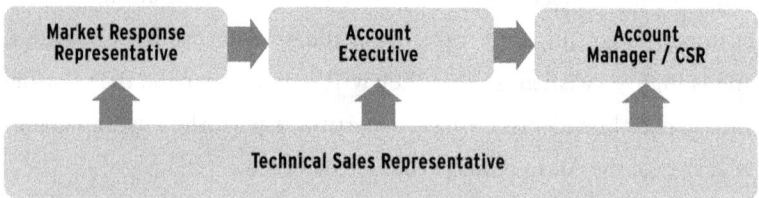

Figure 10: Representative relationships

Creating the ideal sales organisation chart

Now that you understand why you need a team of specialists, and what those specialists are, you need to ensure you structure this team the right way in order to get the best results. If you fail to do this, you're going to waste leads. Leads are expensive to generate, so you need to have the core sales capacity structured correctly to ensure leads are handled effectively.

So, what does the ideal sales structure look like?

First, let's take a quick look at the old structure. In this diagram, you can see the sales team is divided into territories, with each sales group in charge of the end-to-end sales process. The marketing and customer service functions operate independently of the sales team. And there is no specialisation of roles.

Figure 11: Old sales structure

To ensure a future-proof sales function, I recommend building one that reflects the specialist functions required effectively and efficiently engage with the customer at each stage of the customer-driven sales model. Specifically we should develop the following key sales functions:

1　A strong and dedicated prospecting and lead-generation function

2　A strong middle-of-the-funnel core sales function

3　A customer success function

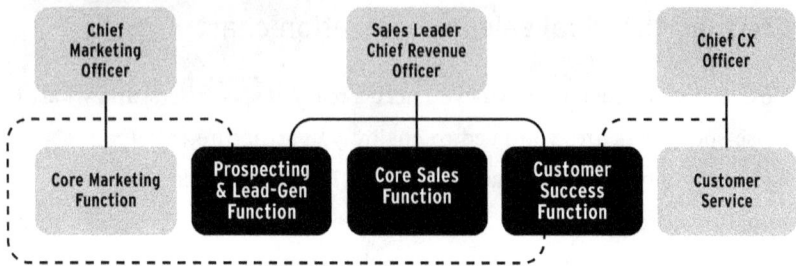

Figure 12: New sales structure

We have broken up the sale leader's responsibilities into three functions, rather than into territories – Prospecting and Lead Generation, Core Sales and Customer Success Function. Rather than the marketing and customer service teams running separately from sales, this structure creates a tight integration between them, with a mix of sales and marketing team members in the Prospecting function (likely with joint management or dotted line responsibilities) and a mix of customer service and sales in the Customer Success (again, with joint management or dotted line responsibilities).

'the single most important thing you can do to improve your sales and lead-generation results is to specialise your roles.'

– AARON ROSS

It follows that the sales roles within these functions need to be specialised in these specific areas. A team of specialists is going to bring greater depth to each of these important disciplines – one that generalist salespeople can't compete with.

Function 1: Prospecting and Lead Generation

This group sits at the top of the funnel and is responsible for creating and developing leads from our target market. This function could be managed directly by the sales head, or the marketing leader, or jointly managed in some form. The key thing is that marketing and sales need to be working closely together at all levels here, and should be focused on the same goals.

The team is made up of inside-based Sales Development Reps, Technical Sales Reps and various marketing specialists. They are all focused on effectively interacting with potential customers in the early stages of their buying journey. They are identifying and prioritising accounts and groups of accounts, and even individual decision makers from various industries and geographies, in order to focus on the more likely prospects.

They are mapping out the customer's buying journey, and making sure we have appropriate content in the right place at the right time when buyers are moving into the market. They are developing and executing outbound strategies towards the priority target accounts to develop and nurture leads.

In addition to Sales Development Reps and Technical Sales Reps, the team should include:

- **Sales Manager**: Manages SDR activity and coaches SDRs.

- **Customer Research and Targeting**: Identifies groups of accounts, ideal customer profiles (ICPs) and specific contact points in target accounts. They will prioritise accounts by analysing the buying potential for our product or service, using a range of data points and market information. They will then deliver this data to SDRs in an efficient and usable form.

- **Content Manager**: Responsible for the overall content strategy and production. To support the sales and marketing teams, content needs to be generated that is relevant to the specific account sets and ICPs being targeted in specific campaigns. The content manager will develop and maintain the content roadmap.

- **Content Producer**: Produces content in line with the content strategy and roadmap.

- **Data Specialist**: Tracks and analyses sales activities across the group and individually. The data specialist also progresses or otherwise against account penetration and campaign goals.

- **Campaign Manager**: Combines the research output, content and sales data to develop and drive campaigns to meet company goals.

Function 2: Core Sales

The core sales team manages the middle of the funnel, and their responsibility is to convert leads into customers. This team is mostly staffed by AEs and their Sales Managers. There will also be some TSRs or SEs, to help with more technical sales and consulting. They could be inside-based, field-based or more likely a mixture of both.

While this team will and should develop some of their own leads through their own network, they will primarily be working on leads developed by the prospecting team, or opportunities that come from existing customers either directly or via the customer success team.

The members of this team will have a strong commercial mindset, be able to present themselves and the company very professionally, and be able to establish credibility and rapport with customers. One key to their success is an understanding and an ability to generate insight into the customer's business.

They will also be expert at helping the buyer build the case for change and fully flesh out the costs of staying with the status quo. This skill should at least be equal with their ability to present the benefits of our products and services.

They will also be expert at helping buyers navigate the internal buying process and the buying committee. Of course, they must have strong negotiation skills that produce deals of great value to both parties.

Within this new sales structure, teamwork and cooperation with the other functions is critical to succeed in these roles. (More on this in Step 6.)

In addition to AEs, Sales Managers and Systems Engineers, the team should include:

- **Inside Sales**: Supports customers and AEs in the ongoing account management and administration of customer accounts, managing quotations, processing orders, tracking deliveries, and so on.

- **Bid Managers**: Expert in writing complex proposals and responding to large company or government bid requests. The Bid Manager will work with the sales team and the various functions in the company to pull together technical information, product information, pricing, and the value proposition.

Function 3: Customer Success

There has been a tide of realisation across B2B businesses that their best source of ongoing revenue and growth is their existing customer base. According to Bain & Company, acquiring a new customer can cost six to seven times more than retaining an existing customer. Furthermore, businesses that boost customer retention rates by as little as five per cent see profit increases ranging from five per cent to ninety-five per cent.

We have also worked out that creating a great customer experience prompts customers to become active advocates for our products and company, and therefore a great source of referrals. But very few companies have changed their sales processes and other structures to take full advantage of these factors.

The customer success function is totally focused on making sure the customer is getting maximum business value from our products and services. It is staffed mostly by Account Managers and/or Customer Success Representatives who are focused on delighting existing customers, and, as a result, driving renewals and business expansion.

Their ultimate goal is to create customer advocates who, through sharing their great customer experiences with other potential customers, will help us break down the doors to new opportunities.

Marketing will also be involved in the customer success group, analysing customer data and identifying opportunities for various products and services, and then developing campaigns for our account base. Ideally, they will also be running campaigns or programs to develop customer advocates, and generating and measuring referrals.

In addition to Account Managers and/or Customer Service Representatives, the team should include:

- **Customer Success Manager**: Proactively works with customers to ensure effective usage of products and meeting of ROI goals. Identifies and may pursue additional sales opportunities, or passes them to the core sales team.

- **Data Specialist**: Tracks and analyses customer usage data, and provides usable and timely intelligence to the sales and customer success teams.

- **Content Manager**: The same duties as described earlier, but with a focus on retention and expansion rather than customer acquisition.

- **Content Producer**: The same duties as described earlier, but with a focus on retention and expansion rather than customer acquisition.

- **Campaign Manager**: The same duties as described earlier, but with a focus on retention and expansion rather than customer acquisition.

Sales Operations and Sales Enablement

Beyond the three core functions are the overarching functions of sales operations and sales enablement.

Sales operations has been around for decades and originally focused on financial analysis, sales reporting and forecasting – providing sales managers with the data needed to run their area of the business. However, over time this function has evolved to have a much wider and strategic role focused on overall sales effectiveness. It will often encompass sales planning, sales processes, sales systems, technology, training, compensation, territory management, deal management and pricing as well as the traditional reporting, analysis and forecasting functions. This takes a huge workload from sales managers, enabling them to focus on key selling activities and managing their people.

In my recommended sales structure, the role of sales operations is to study how the sales function is performing at a granular level and determine how to improve key metrics, including call and activity metrics, close rates, average deal sizes, deal profitability, the selling and admin time ratio, pipeline metrics, forecasting and forecast accuracy, usage of technology tools and more. This function can be a tremendous resource for sales leaders, especially in larger teams, to keep track of what's happening across the business and correct any underperformance.

Sales enablement, on the other hand, is relatively new and the term is sometimes used interchangeably with sales operations. Tamara Schenk, the Research Director at CSO Insights and co-author of the book *Sales Enablement*, gives the following definition of the sales enablement function: 'Sales enablement is a collaborative, strategic discipline that's designed to increase predictable sales results by providing consistent and scalable enablement services for all customer-facing roles and managers so they can create value in every single buyer interaction.'

This definition demonstrates that sales enablement does overlap with sales operations, but goes beyond the responsibilities outlined for the operations function. With the challenges facing modern B2B sales teams, the sales enablement function has emerged to assist the sales team in more effectively engaging with customers.

Historically, the sales team would have received training in their company's products and services and received collateral from marketing, and then been left to their own devices to figure out how to approach the customer. The challenge would be if the information was contradictory, out of alignment with sales goals or irrelevant when it came to the real-life scenarios salespeople faced in the field. This created a gap between the support functions and sales – a gap that sales enablement fills.

One of sales enablement's key focuses is to understand the target customers and their buying journeys, and then coordinate with all of the key supporting and training functions in order to deliver messaging, materials and processes that will be effective in their specific territories. Sales enablement then measures sales effectiveness as a result of their initiatives. They will measure if salespeople are getting better results throughout the sales process, such as securing more first meetings or discovery calls, as well as the end results of the process, such as average sale values, sales cycle times, the portion of salespeople and territories meeting quota, and so on.

Beyond the coordination of training and materials, and the reporting on results, sales enablement also takes ownership for the sales technology stack. As I covered in Part 1, the number of opportunities and tools available to support sales has exploded recently. The sales enablement function is in a good position to analyse what will work best for the sales team, monitor and drive adoption, and ultimately improve sales effectiveness as a result.

Sales operations and enablement have progressed enormously in the past few years and must be considered for any vendor business that is developing and improving its overall sales function. Careful investments in these areas can have a big impact on the effectiveness and productivity of your whole sales team.

7 key benefits of the new sales structure

By implementing the new sales structure, we will build a more sophisticated business. Instead of just having our pipeline and sales results to drive the business, we will have control over a whole range of inputs and outputs around our business.

Namely, a prospecting and lead-gen machine with lots of levers and variables, a strong core sales function that will efficiently progress deals and secure profitable outcomes, and a customer retention and expansion function that will nurture our customers for a healthy long-term relationship.

Here are seven specific benefits of the new sales structure.

1. Experts at each customer touchpoint

In the traditional sales model, generalist salespeople have huge variance in their abilities. For example, they may be great at prospecting but not great at managing ongoing relationships. They may be great at developing insight and negotiation, but aren't skilled at generating new leads.

And in an increasingly competitive, complex sales environment, with so many tools and techniques to master in each of these areas, it's difficult to imagine a team of generalists being exceptional across the board.

In contrast, when we work together within the specialised functions of prospecting, core sales and customer success, and focus on being world-class in our specific areas, we are going to be much more effective in generating leads, developing new customers, and then growing our customer relationships in the long term.

2. A more consistent and steady business

Even if we have some sales superstars who are great at all the key sales functions, they will inevitably be drawn towards one or two areas at a time, and neglect the other critical functions. This creates unevenness in activity, leading to a less stable, less manageable business.

For instance, if a generalist salesperson is working on some large deals, this can be all-consuming. As a result, they may drop their prospecting activity or stop taking good care of existing customers. In another scenario, a salesperson may find themselves in a situation where some of their large clients consume all of their time, leaving little time for prospecting or prioritising new opportunities.

We are all familiar with the feast-and-famine sales territories where things look like they are going well, with a few big deals closing or large customers buying. Then all of a sudden sales drop, and the sales team is scrambling to generate prospecting activity and recover business.

In the traditional sales model, when business is going well, prospecting naturally takes a back seat. In contrast, the new structure allows for very consistent, high-quality activity in all the key sales functions. This should result in a steadier, more manageable and less stressful operation.

3. Earlier engagement with customers

The prospecting and lead-gen function in particular addresses a major challenge for salespeople today. That is, accessing customers efficiently and getting enough pipeline.

We have already discussed at length the changed customer buying journey, and the fact that customers are not engaging with suppliers until they are well advanced in their buying research. Having a specialised function made up of sales *and* marketing experts – who understand the new customer journey, and are engaging with customers when, where and how they want to be engaged – is a huge benefit.

It allows us to engage earlier than the core sales function, and establish our company and products as a credible solution for their business problem. By the time they are ready to engage, they should be well qualified and positive towards us, in addition to being very well informed.

We should be generating a steady and predictable flow of qualified leads for our core sales team. There is a lot of talent in this specific field – it's really exciting to set this function up and see the results flow in.

4. Improved cost structure and productivity

Over the past couple of centuries, specialisation of tasks has been applied to most industries, but not so much to the sales function. Having whole teams and individual team members focus on fewer tasks is going to boost efficiency and therefore deliver a cost benefit, as we are getting more output for the same or a lower cost.

But on top of that, we will also be utilising the latest tools and tech to generate more productivity. Further, we will move more and more of the sales process from field roles to inside sales roles and towards online wherever we can. This will also generate cost savings.

5. Continuous improvement

When all salespeople are performing all the sales functions end-to-end, it's much harder to drive improvement across the business. Each rep is likely following their own methods and processes to get results, which makes it difficult to better understand the prospecting process across the business, or the approach to customer expansion. It also makes it difficult to see what is (or isn't) working and to make improvements, since every salesperson is probably doing things slightly differently.

Having specialist teams focused on narrower functions makes it easier to create standardised processes within those teams and to drive meaningful improvements at each stage of the sales process, since it is already broken down into more manageable parts.

6. Sales development opportunities

Having many more specialised roles offers a range of interesting and varied options for those in the team wanting to grow themselves and their skillsets. Instead of sales reps just looking to become sales managers, or an inside salesperson looking to become a field AE, there are many more options. A salesperson with an interest in lead generation and content could move into a content marketing role, while another one with an interest in data and analytics might want to move into campaign management, for instance.

Providing an interesting career path has been a challenge in many sales organisations in the past, but now we can offer a range of stimulating specialised roles.

7. High visibility of key metrics

All of these benefits will add up to a healthier business with much better visibility. In other words, we won't just be looking at sales outcomes at the macro level, without really understanding the underlying contributions from the various components of our sales process.

Before, we would be looking at forecasts and pipeline reports at a territory level, or even as an individual sales rep, but not really understanding the status of our lead generation or prospecting activity, how well we were converting leads into deals, how we were progressing on our customer retention and expansion programs, and so on. As a result, it was difficult to tweak these specific activities accurately.

With our new sales structure, we will have high visibility of our success or otherwise at each stage of the customer journey and be able to take effective corrective action.

Making the new structure work for smaller teams

You might think the new sales structure only works in large-scale organisations, but it can definitely work in small businesses too. I have seen very effective specialised sales functions work at small scale.

For example, I was recently working with the Australian division of a US multinational technology company, which was launching into a new product category with an entirely new set of customers. They had a group of four B2B salespeople, who were initially tasked with penetrating this new market sector. But after a while, they realised they weren't able to get the penetration in the accounts, nor were they meeting with the key people they wanted to connect with.

With all of the other responsibilities the salespeople were carrying, they just weren't able to allocate the time and effort to get this right. We added a dedicated SDR to target the specific accounts we were after, and allocated some marketing resource (in the form of a part-time marketing role) to help with the content and communication strategy.

Within a month, we had identified many of the key decision makers, opened many conversations, and were starting to generate meetings and real opportunities for the sales team. Within a year, the strategy had paid off, with several multimillion-dollar deals secured.

The same rule applies to the customer success function. It doesn't require an entire team and a dedicated manager to make it work. You can start with a single person or part of a person's time. Maybe focus on your top customers or your newest customers, or customers with the highest growth potential first, and see what results you get. Straightaway, there will be less load on the core sales team, so they'll have more time to spend on developing and closing business. In addition, you should achieve higher customer satisfaction levels and strong referrals.

Here's an example of a small change I made recently with a small client, who was keen to see more consistent focus on prospecting and lead generation in their business. The client's old sales structure had four AEs, each supported by an inside salesperson, with all sales activity in the territory being managed by both of them.

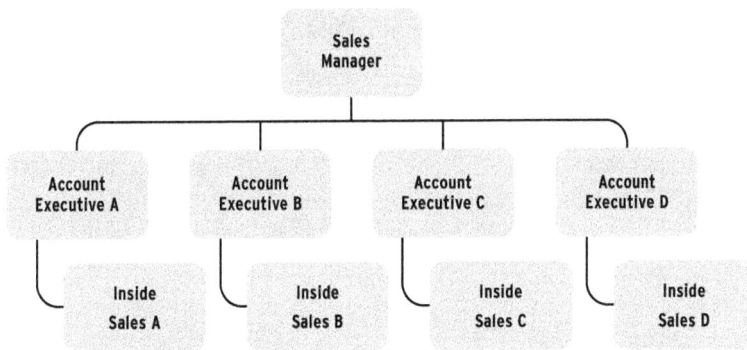

Figure 13: Old structure, small team

The challenge was achieving a consistent level of prospecting activity. We made a small change by converting one of the inside salespeople to an SDR, dedicated to prospecting and lead generation, with the remaining three inside salespeople focused on supporting the AEs on deal-making activities and managing existing customers.

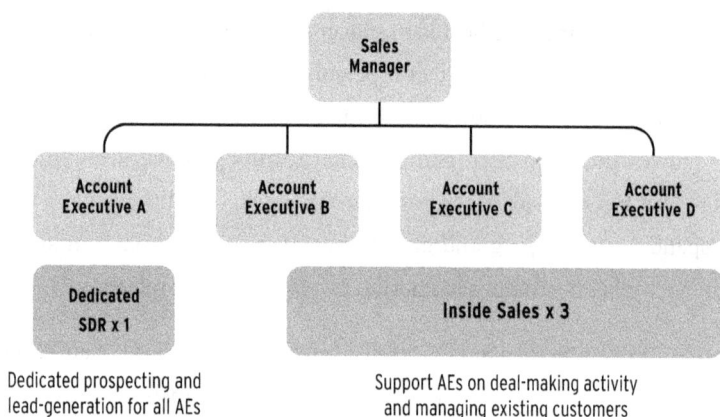

Figure 14: New structure, small team

Some of the benefits from this change include:

- Consistent level of prospecting activity into the key target accounts
- Clear visibility of prospecting activity and lead-generation outcomes
- Improvement and refinement of our prospecting approach
- A great career opportunity for the inside salesperson to move laterally into a different and higher profile role
- One to two major leads being generated each week

SUMMARY

That brings us to the end of Step 1. Before we move on to Step 2, here's a list of the key points to remember:

- Buyer behaviour has changed, customers are harder to reach, and they have high expectations of salespeople and of the whole customer experience. It is critical that we shift our structure to meet this challenge. In essence, there needs to be a shift from the traditional sales model to a customer-driven sales model.

- Traditional sales models had a focus on driving customers through the sales organisation's sales process and forcing deals to meet quarterly targets. The new model is more customer-driven and recognises that customers want to conduct their buying journey more independently.

- Instead of a sales structure built purely on territories, we need to build specialist sales functions with deep individual capabilities. This will allow us to effectively and efficiently engage with the customer at each stage of the customer journey. Specifically we build functions that focus on: prospecting and lead generation; managing the core, middle-of-the-funnel sales activities; and creating customer advocates and boosting referral selling.

- The marketing and customer experience functions are key business partners in the success of the new model. While sales can still lead the key sales-generating functions, it is critical that we partner fully and leverage these stakeholders to achieve the maximum result for our company.

- Implementing the new sales structure will lead to a more sophisticated business. Instead of just having our pipeline and sales results to drive our business, we will have control over a whole range of inputs and outputs around our business.

- The new sales structure is not just applicable to large-scale organisations. It can also work with smaller teams. Having a single employee focused on prospecting activity or customer success can make a big difference to your business.

Step 2: Recruit and Promote the Right Talent

'Great vision without great people is irrelevant.'

JIM COLLINS

If I had to choose one big initiative from this book for you to prioritise and execute, this would be it. I believe that following the advice in this step will significantly lift your sales performance, even if you don't change anything else.

Imagine if every team member in your current sales structure was excelling in their role, highly satisfied with the type of work they were doing, and committed to staying with the company for the long term.

Think of the difference that would make to the organisation as a whole. It would be amazing, wouldn't it? However, in every team, we know there are areas where it's just not working and, no matter how hard we coach people or try to fix things, the issues persist.

This leads to a whole host of larger, ongoing problems, including high staff turnover. According to Leadership IQ, forty-six per cent of all new hires fail within eighteen months. For executive new hires, the failure rate is even higher at fifty-eight per cent. Meanwhile, IBM says thirty-nine per cent of hiring managers regret their decision and wouldn't re-hire, while only nineteen per cent of new hires achieve 'unequivocal success', according to Leadership IQ.

It's also much harder and costlier to address people-fit problems once they occur. Studies estimate the cost of losing an employee is one and a half to two times their salary. This includes recruitment costs (screening, interviewing and hiring), onboarding costs and training costs.

46%

The portion of new hires who fail within the first 18 months

In the sales profession, the loss is usually even higher, costing a B2B business in actual sales as well. Ramp time to a reasonable level of sales productivity differs depending on the product and industry, but will generally be in the range of four to eight months.

Even at that point, the new hire is unlikely to be producing at the same level as salespeople with two to five years' tenure. According to CSO Insights, sixty-seven per cent of companies say it takes seven months or more for new salespeople to become fully productive, with forty-seven per cent saying it takes ten months or more.

This chart is a simple representation of the difference between a new sales hire and a tenured salesperson.

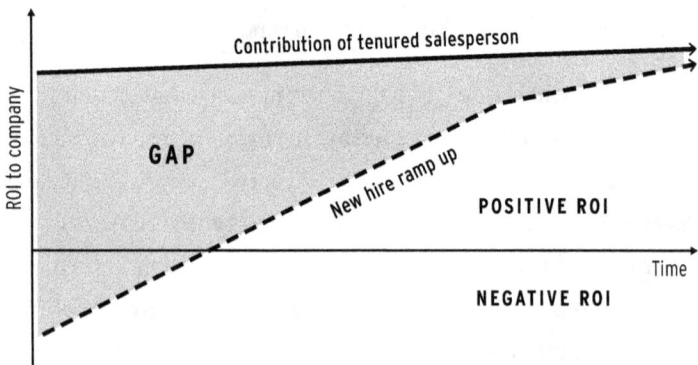

Figure 15: Contribution of tenured salesperson versus new hire

There are a few key points to remember here:

- New hires are a negative drag on our ROI in the early stages

- Tenured salespeople just keep getting more productive year after year

- Even as the new hires start generating positive ROI, there is still an opportunity cost compared to the tenured performer

- This is why it is so important to get the right people in the right roles, where they will be successful and therefore want to stay with the organisation for a long time. By putting in the effort upfront, we can massively improve our staff turnover and boost our sales results.

It's an unfortunate fact, but some of your current team members may not fit into the new sales structure outlined in Step 1. If you think about the way salespeople operated traditionally, their activities were very much centred on relationship building; building professional and even personal relationships with key customers. This was often done via wining and dining, golfing, sporting matches and so on.

But in the new sales environment, this is just not enough – or even necessary – to keep the customer happy. As we've already discussed, buyers prefer to research products and services on their own, and are actively *avoiding* engaging with salespeople until they have to.

We now have more specialised sales roles, and each of these roles requires different skills and attributes. If we are looking for A-level performance in each function – which is what customers have come to expect – we need to be more careful and consistent in how we assess and select staff.

1.5–2X salary
is the cost of a failed hire

To address the talent issue, we need to look at both our existing staff as well as properly vet any new hires. Fortunately, we can use the same methods for both of these tasks – structured interviewing, profiling and assessment tests, and the creation of clearly defined development opportunities and career paths. Those are the topics we'll discuss in this step.

Unstructured interviews versus structured interviews

Before we discuss the benefits and practicalities of structured interviews, it's important to understand the pitfalls of unstructured interviews.

An unstructured interview is done somewhat informally, like a conversation, where the interviewer is trying to get to know the candidate. The questions tend to be open-ended and are not fixed in advance, so the discussion can head in different directions, depending on the interviewee's answers and where the interviewer wants to take the discussion.

Questions might include:

- Can you tell me a bit about yourself?
- How would your previous employer describe you?
- What are your career goals?
- What are your strengths and weaknesses?
- The problem with unstructured interviews is that they're an extremely poor way of assessing and selecting sales talent.

In 1998, Frank Schmidt and John Hunter published a meta-analysis of eighty-five years' research on how well different assessment techniques predict performance. They looked at nineteen different assessment techniques in total, and found that unstructured interviews can explain only fourteen per cent of an employee's performance. This is ahead of reference checks (seven per cent) and years of work experience (three per cent), but not much else.

Another study ranked the unstructured interview the lowest of any tool used in the selection process – between five per cent and fifteen per cent predictive – so, at best, about one in every six interviews will be accurate in identifying the 'real' person.

Then there's the issue of bias, which is common in unstructured interviews, and can have a very negative impact on our hiring decisions. There are various forms of bias, including:

- **Appearance bias**. Interviewers are greatly influenced by someone's appearance, their clothing, their manner, their grooming, their attractiveness, their greeting and so forth. They feel that they can judge someone's character or personality from their appearance, when these characteristics have little or nothing to do with the ability of the candidate to perform the role.

- **First impression bias**. People are hugely swayed by first impressions. There's a famous research project by the University of Toledo that videotaped a series of job interviews. The interviews were conducted by two trained interviewers, who completed a post-interview questionnaire, evaluating the candidates on their interview performance, behaviour, rapport and professional skills.

  Brief video clips were then shown to naïve observers, who only watched the initial twenty seconds of each video, and were then asked to rate each interviewee on twelve personal attributes, including competence and warmth. The university found the 'trained' interviewers' first impressions of job candidates were the same as those of the naïve observers.

- **Contrast effect**. This happens when a stronger candidate interviews right before or after a weak candidate, and we will get an impression that they are well qualified. But while they appear good compared to the other candidate, they still may not be qualified or be the best person for the role.

- **Stereotyping**. This is where the interviewer forms an opinion based on the candidate's gender, religion, race, age or any other such characteristic.

- **Similarity bias**. Managers often hire people just like themselves. Maybe this comes from a conscious or unconscious bias towards people with the same characteristics. But this doesn't help develop a team with diverse strengths and opinions, nor find us the best person for the job.

- **Overly sensitive to negative information**. Often a small amount of negative information will distort the interviewer's whole impression of the candidate. People are likely to weigh negative information more than positive information.

- **Halo effect bias**. This is where one great achievement from the candidate overshadows everything else about them. The interviewer somehow relates to a candidate's specific achievement and tends to favour them as a result.

- **Outsized influence of likeability and rapport building**. This is where the candidate attempts to find shared interests or mutual acquaintances with the interviewer – in an attempt to form a quick connection – and the interviewer lets it cloud their judgement.

In light of all that, why do we persist with unstructured interviewing?

Most hirers are unaware of, or just don't buy into the validity of, the research on the ineffectiveness of unstructured interviewing. Instead, they back their ability to 'see through' candidates or 'read' candidates.

It's also worth noting that the traditional interview process is an ingrained part of the way many companies operate. Senior managers and recruiters have been conducting interviews for years, and many truly believe they know what they are doing. They have developed their interviewing approach, and are confident to make assessments using their interview skills and their experience. But while some may be effective using unstructured interviews, the statistics show the vast majority are not.

What's the alternative? Structured interviews.

Structured interviews occur where candidates are asked a consistent set of questions with clear criteria to assess the quality of each candidate's responses. There are two kinds of structured interviews: behavioural and situational.

Behavioural interviews ask candidates to describe prior achievements and match those to what is required in the current job ('Can you tell me about a time when you achieved X?'). Situational interviews present a job-related hypothetical situation ('What would you do if X happened?'). A diligent interviewer will probe deeply to assess the veracity and thought process behind the stories told by the candidate.

According to a study conducted by Frank Schmidt and John Hunter, moving to a structured interview process can improve our success rate from fourteen per cent to fifty per cent. If we add psychometric testing to the mix (more on this in the next section), we can achieve a seventy-five per cent success rate.

So how can you run a successful structured interview? Here are some tips to get started:

- List six to eight key performance factors, or competencies, for a position. One or two behaviourally based interview questions should be developed for each performance factor.

- Ask every candidate the same behavioural questions, based on the job competencies.

- Create specific job descriptions before the hiring process commences, and keep them up to date. These should form the basis for the structured interview competencies.

- Rate each aspect of the selection process, particularly the interview, and make the ratings descriptive, particularly for each job requirement (for example, 'exceeds', 'meets', 'does not meet' and so on).

- Finally, always use two or more interviewers. The intended purpose of a job interview is to gather information about the candidate in order for us to make a judgement call and subsequent hire, or non-hire, decision. When job interviews are carried out by a single interviewer, there is more chance for bias, which affects the outcome. That's why it's important to always use at least two interviewers.

Profiling and assessment tests

In the previous section, I touched briefly on psychometric testing. Psychometric tests are a standard and scientific method used to measure individuals' mental capabilities and behavioural style. They are designed to assess candidates' suitability for a role based on the required personality characteristics and aptitude.

Psychometric tests are just one assessment tool we can use to more accurately evaluate a job candidate. Other types include cognitive tests – which measure a candidate's reasoning, memory and knowledge of a specific role function – and simulation tests, which test candidates in real-life work environment situations.

Using a sales assessment test – rather than relying on gut feeling, which is a purely subjective and emotional form of assessment – can help us avoid making bad hiring decisions. It can also lead to significant cost savings.

PredictiveHire, a SaaS solutions provider, observed that one of its clients could have saved $1.1 million by using an assessment tool. This client had hired eighty people over twelve months. Without using a sales assessment test, it cost them an additional $800,000 in time to screen and interview the eighty candidates.

In addition to cutting costs, sales assessment tests decrease hiring time. For example, hotel giant Hilton has cut its recruiting cycle down from six weeks to five *days*, simply by using data-driven assessment methods. Hilton's sales assessment test has trimmed the number of interview questions from 200 to just five. It has also increased the chance of hiring someone after one face-to-face interview.

Despite the proven success of sales assessment tools, only twenty-nine per cent of business leaders are leveraging these emerging technology options, according to Peak Sales Recruiting, even though just six per cent think their current process works well for them.

So, why don't more companies use these tools? Well, for starters, they are hard to develop. You have to create them, test them, and make sure interviewers stick to them. And then you have to continually refresh them, so candidates don't compare notes and come prepared with all the answers. It's a lot of work, but the alternative is to waste time and money with a traditional hiring process that is either highly subjective or discriminatory, or both, and therefore inefficient.

If you're not sure where to start, perhaps you can take some inspiration from Unilever, which has combined video interviewing and gaming (yes, you read that right) to create a digital, four-step recruiting process.

Here's how it works:

1 Candidates complete a short online form associated with their LinkedIn profile. They receive a text message almost immediately after completing the form.

2 Candidates spend twenty minutes playing a series of games, which gives Unilever insight into different capabilities and traits, including personality, communication style and problem-solving skills. After completing these games, candidates receive feedback within forty-eight hours.

3 A program called Pymetrics selects eligible candidates to move forward. These candidates go through a video interviewing process, conducted by HireVue. The HireVue software assesses the interviews and ranks the candidates based on their fit for the role.

4   The highest ranked candidates are invited to Unilever's Discovery Centre where they participate in activities they would be expected to perform on a daily basis.

This four-step process has decreased Unilever's hiring time from four months to two weeks, and as short as one to two days. Unilever's recruiters now screen two candidates and put only one through the four-step recruiting process, rather than screening six candidates to select one for a face-to-face interview. This has reduced recruiter screening time by seventy-five per cent.

And there are many sales-specific assessment tools out there now. Two that I have used with success are SalesGenomix and Perception People Analytics.

SalesGenomix is an easy-to-access and simple-to-use online sales assessment, which draws on data from over 500,000 sales professionals to determine the traits of the most successful. It also distinguishes between fourteen different sales roles so is a good one-stop shop.

Perception People Analytics has developed a full employee and candidate intelligence system. It combines KPI performance for specific roles with detailed testing to find the key correlations between employees' attributes and their performance in specific functions of specific roles. The system utilises machine learning, so it becomes more accurate as it takes in more performance data.

These tools can help us identify and measure desirable traits for successful salespeople, as well as any undesirable traits. For example, here's a snapshot generated by Perception People Analytics, showing the performance rating for an SDR, with a breakdown of their desirable and undesirable traits and a prediction of how they will perform the key tasks required in the SDR role (these include making calls, setting meetings and so on). In addition to helping sales leaders with hiring decisions, these tools can help leaders better manage individuals and teams by delivering a better understanding of individuals' strengths and weaknesses.

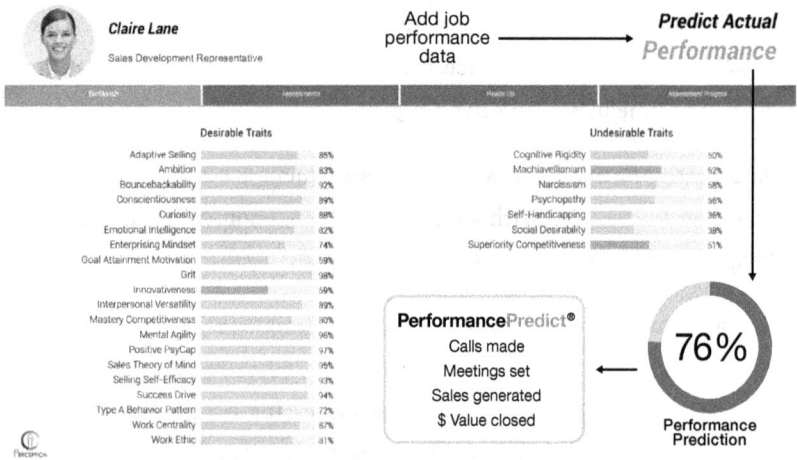

Figure 16: Enterprise Sales Snapshot, Source: People Perception Analytics

Brett Morris, CEO and founder of People Perception Analytics, shares the following comment: 'When you synthesise the vast amount of data around interviewing, it shows that interviews are notoriously unreliable, they are subject to personal biases and attitude fraud, and even the FBI with their advanced techniques find it hard to detect if someone is embellishing the truth, so it's really hard to work that out in an interview. But sales leaders, hiring managers, recruiters can get access to granular data about a candidate that gives them an insight into the makeup of the individual and whether they have the right makeup for a particular sales role. For example, there are certain characteristics we want for a lead-generation role, and there are certain types of people that just shouldn't be in that type of role, but it will be hard to really find that out just through interviewing.'

If someone doesn't have the core attributes required for a particular role, it is hard to get good performance from them. While some traits can be improved, many can't, which means it doesn't matter how much coaching you give them, or how much pressure you put on them to perform. I can think of many instances where I have seen someone drowning in their role, simply because they weren't suited to it. This can have a devastating impact on the individual, the team, and the organisation as a whole. And it is so hard to uncover this information in an interview, especially in an unstructured interview.

Now that sales roles are becoming more specialised, it's even more important to ensure the people we are hiring and promoting have the right traits and skills to excel in those roles. Profiling and assessment tests help to ensure this.

Creating development opportunities and career paths

As we discussed at the start of Step 2, tenure is a huge driver of performance in the sales profession. This is why staff retention is so important to our overall sales performance. Keeping the top talent happy is particularly important, since top performers make an outsize contribution to our results. In a study of top tech firms, Doctor John Sullivan found high-performing employees contribute between ten and 1,000 times more value than average employees. Just consider the following numbers from his survey of top-performing companies.

Difference in performance between average performers and high performers in the same role	
Netflix & Yahoo	10X
Apple	25X
Google	300X
Microsoft	1,000X

Figure 17: Performance variation at leading tech companies

However, the competition for top talent is intense. It's not enough for high performers to get paid well and have a nice work environment. They want challenges and growth opportunities. They want to learn more, be challenged, take on more responsibilities and different assignments, and be given the chance to reach their full potential. If they're not moving forward and developing, they'll be unhappy and may even go elsewhere.

According to a Gallup survey, when ninety-three per cent of workers advanced in their careers, it was by taking a job at another company. Just seven per cent took on new opportunities within their current organisations. Meanwhile, an APA survey found that while sixty-one per cent of employees said their employer offered development and career opportunities, roughly half of those surveyed said their employer didn't provide career development activities sufficient for advancement.

By failing to provide such opportunities, you risk losing your top talent. This lowers morale among the rest of team, and it also hurts profits. The top ten per cent of your salespeople produce eighty per cent of the profit, and more than half of the actual sales. So you need to do whatever you can to keep them around – and keep them satisfied.

Thankfully, with the specialist roles required as part of the new sales structure discussed in Step 1, there is no shortage of career development opportunities for your top performers.

Sales advancement opportunities were more limited in the traditional model. We had generalist salespeople working in specific territories and reporting to sales managers, so top performers would always look to the sales manager role to expand their knowledge and skillset, and their income.

Then when we supplemented field sales with inside sales, there was another element of opportunity. Namely, the inside sales team could aspire to become field salespeople, but rarely the other way around. And field salespeople might move to an inside sales manager role as a stepping stone to becoming a regional sales manager or the overall sales leader.

Now with so many specialised roles, there are lots of opportunities to give our salespeople varied and exciting assignments. Often people aren't suited to or interested in more seniority, but do look for change and challenge. Lateral moves provide that.

So, in this context, how do we best manage career pathing and development? We use the same methods outlined earlier for the hiring process – structured interviewing, and profiling and assessment tests.

There is a great opportunity to optimise the team function by encouraging individuals to strive for lateral as well as vertical career progression. If we put the right people into the right roles, where their innate talent and interests match the role, they will be successful.

We must avoid the pitfalls of giving someone a role just because they want it. We must ensure they are suited to it, using the processes described in the previous sections. Also, as hiring can take three to four months, we should always be ready in advance. This means being aware of early warning signs of possible attrition in your team, including:

- **Performance**. If, after receiving feedback and coaching, an employee continues to show poor performance, this usually indicates they are not capable enough for the role, or don't want to do it.

- **Attitude**. If an employee has a poor attitude towards their own work and a low level of professionalism, and/or a poor attitude as part of the team, it could be because they are looking elsewhere.

- **Adapting to change**. As we know, what worked yesterday won't necessarily lead to success today. We all need to be constantly improving and adapting. A resistance to change suggests a lack of engagement and possible attrition.

I often say that to be below our sales capacity is a crime, and I have always made it a top priority as a sales leader to ensure I minimise the number of empty seats on my teams. Every empty seat is carrying a quota, so every day we have an open role it is hurting our performance and putting pressure on the leader and the rest of the team.

While we do not want to be rushing our hiring, as the consequences are even worse than leaving a position open, this can be managed by building a pipeline of high-quality candidates. When you have a strong pipeline of talent, you'll have more confidence to manage the team strongly, and without compromising your standards. If you have no pipeline, you could face a three- to four-month talent gap, during which time you're likely to relax your performance standards, not to mention miss your sales targets. This is not good for the organisation's overall performance. It also eats away at the morale of your team, especially your top performers. So, make sure you're always in a position to make changes on your own terms.

THE COST OF POOR PROMOTIONS

Giving someone a promotion just because they want it can have disastrous consequences. Just think of the possible implications of taking a great salesperson and putting them in charge of a team only for it not to work out. Just some of these include:

The team loses a great salesperson, and the business they were bringing in.

Relationships with this salesperson's customers are disrupted.

If the salesperson doesn't perform well as a manager, this then impacts the morale and job satisfaction for the entire team.

When they move on, the business has to recruit someone else for the role. This is costly, time-consuming and risky.

It is a hard decision to reverse, as often the failing manager won't want to take their old job or go back to their old salary.

The person may leave the company altogether.

With all of these potential costs and downsides to the business, it's important to be very considered and run a robust process before any significant promotion. Here again is a great case for applying structured interviews and profiling tools to help us if folks are ready for promotion.

SUMMARY

That brings us to the end of Step 2. Before we move on to Step 3, here's a list of the key points to remember:

- Forty-six per cent of all new hires fail within eighteen months. For executive new hires, the failure rate is even higher at fifty-eight per cent.

- To address talent issues, we need to look at both our existing staff as well as properly vet any new hires. We can use the same methods for both of these tasks – structured interviewing, profiling and assessment tests, and creating clearly defined development opportunities and career paths.

- Unstructured interviews are an extremely poor way of assessing and selecting sales talent, partly due to various forms of bias, including appearance bias and first impression bias. Structured interviews are a better alternative.

- There are two kinds of structured interviews: behavioural and situational. Behavioural interviews ask candidates to describe prior achievements and match those to what is required in the current job, while situational interviews present a job-related hypothetical situation.

- Psychometric tests are a standard and scientific method used to measure individuals' mental capabilities and behavioural style. They are designed to assess candidates' suitability for a role based on the required personality characteristics and aptitude.

- High-performing employees can contribute between ten and 1,000 times more value than average employees. For this reason, keeping the top talent happy is very important.

- To create clearly defined development opportunities and career paths, we can use the same methods as we do for hiring – structured interviewing, and profiling and assessment tests. We should avoid giving someone a role just because they want it and promoting the wrong person is very costly.

Step 3: Develop Red-Hot Lead-Gen Capability

'Proper prospecting prevents poverty.'

JEFFREY GITOMER

As we know, customers are much harder to reach nowadays than they were in the past. They avoid salespeople until later in the sales process, they have many other reliable sources of information, and they value other information sources more than salespeople. On top of this, incumbent suppliers are aggressively implementing CX initiatives and doing their best to protect their account base. This means effective prospecting is harder than it used to be, and requires new skills and significant teamwork with marketing.

The generalist salesperson is at a massive disadvantage nowadays. It takes a dedicated and professional approach, utilising all of the latest tools and techniques, to reach buyers effectively and start influencing them early in their buying journey. The prospecting and lead-gen process requires constant re-evaluation and evolution. We need to always be looking over the horizon for the next big thing – we need to be watching the trends on our returns for existing processes, and constantly testing out new ones.

Once something starts to waver, we need to reinvent our approach again. For example, sellers who adopted social selling early on had some great success – there are plenty of consultants on LinkedIn and elsewhere touting how they achieved ten times the prospecting results using this method. Now social is getting pretty crowded, and the only way to succeed is to make it part of an overall contact strategy.

With this in mind, it's impossible for the generalist salesperson to singlehandedly keep up with the constant changes taking place in the industry and in prospecting methods. It also leads to constant cycles of feast and famine. This chart shows what typically happens with generalist salespeople when they're put into a new territory.

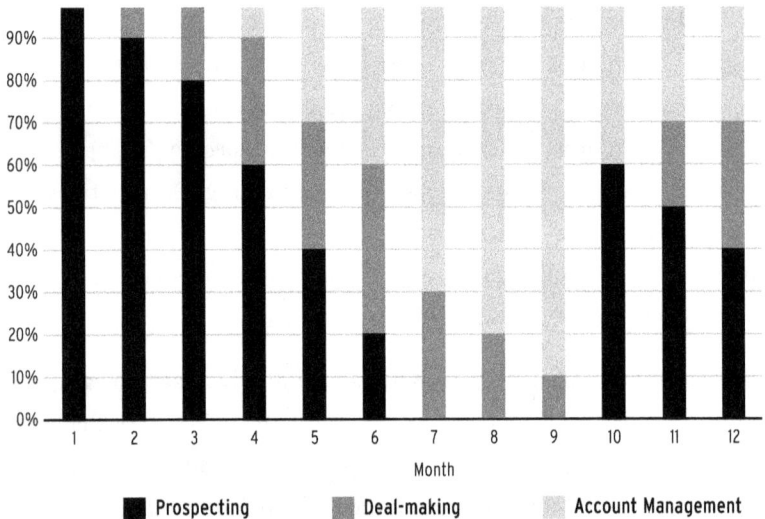

Figure 18: Generalist salesperson time allocation

At the beginning, they dedicate all their time to prospecting. After a while, they start generating some leads, and therefore need to allocate some time to working on and closing those deals. They must then devote some time to keeping these customers happy – this is where the account management comes in. Before long, though, they have created enough business and activity with existing customers that no prospecting happens for a while, and therefore the deal activity starts dropping off too.

In this example we see that around month ten, as happens in real life to many salespeople, a couple of big customers go quiet or stop buying altogether, so now we have to start driving our prospecting activity again. And the whole cycle starts all over again.

Having our prospecting and lead-generation activities dispersed through the entire sales team – and all mixed in with other activities at the individual level – simply doesn't work. As indicated in the chart, prospecting activity is likely to fall by the wayside as other pressures come to bear. But if we have a dedicated prospecting and lead-gen function, as recommended in Step 1, we eliminate this risk.

It's important to note that there are four main sources of prospects in the context of B2B sales:

- **Outbound lead activity**. This is the focus of this step. It's where we have a team proactively targeting and reaching out to our target customers. This is a key sales function, staffed by sales and marketing people. It is occasionally owned by marketing, but is typically the responsibility of the sales leader.

- **Inbound lead activity**. Inbound leads come from marketing activities, which are almost exclusively run and owned by the marketing team. Instead of reaching out to prospects, the marketing team lays out a trail of information and incentives (in the form of content, such as a blog) that prospects can follow towards your company.

- **Prospecting activity**. This is where the members of the core sales team leverage their networks and industry relationships, and expand on their relationships with existing customers.

- **Referrals from existing customers**. This is where existing customers refer your product or service to other potential customers. Referrals are one of the most powerful selling and marketing tools available. We will cover this component of lead generation in a later step.

This step will focus on outbound lead activity. While many sales leaders are advocating a focus towards inbound lead-gen, the result is that they are neglecting outbound, which is leaving a lot of opportunity on the table (and available for competitors). Consequently, in this step I will cover the importance of quality versus quantity, warm calling, account-based marketing, lead scoring and management, inside sales, and the sales technology stack.

Quality vs quantity: The cornerstone of any successful lead-gen function

While many organisations have realised they need a dedicated prospecting function and have put a lot of resources into it, few are getting the results they want. Many have been disappointed with their returns, while others initially achieved some good results but the returns declined over time.

The reason for this is that the focus is on top-down of outbound metrics – the number of calls, emails, social contacts, and meetings or discovery calls. Unfortunately, with so many companies setting up these outbound, quantity-obsessed SDR teams, customers are becoming overwhelmed by the noise, making it extremely difficult to cut through.

There are so many studies that show that it is taking more and more calls or contacts to get a prospect to respond.

Jordan Mara is the founder of Coho Sales Consulting, the world's leading sales enablement business for SaaS start-ups, and faces this problem regularly in his work. He gives the following example, 'I was called in by a North American SaaS company to look at their prospecting efforts. They had five SDRs and had made over 30,000 contacts (phone, email, social) in a quarter, but were totally missing their sales results and outcomes.'

This is exactly why many sales leaders, field sales teams and other business leaders are sceptical about creating a dedicated prospecting team. In Jordan's example, the team performed a huge amount of activity, but because their focus was the quantity of contacts, they largely generated low-quality leads which had a poor conversion rate.

It doesn't have to be this way. In fact, prospecting teams can work exceptionally well if they are directed in the right way.

Jordan is expert on modern prospecting and has helped many companies get their prospecting efforts on track. He suggests the following overall approach.

1 **Narrow the account universe upfront.** The key is not simply bringing in as many leads as possible, but prioritising the accounts that are the best fit for our offering – those that match the ICP. This might include prioritising by industry, company size, location, trigger events and other relevant criteria.

Nobody should be reaching out to a prospect that's outside their ICP. Before doing any outbound prospecting, we should first be asking, 'Who are our customers? Who are we adding value to? Who is renewing with us?' Track down the individuals in the key roles in those accounts who would benefit most from your solution.

2 **Systematically research those individuals and companies.** Gather what you can about these prospects from their company website, their LinkedIn profile and across the web. Then customise and personalise your approach to each individual with what Jordan calls the 4Cs:

- **Company**. We can personalise it based off something about the **company**. So, if we were selling a SaaS solution for managing hospital records and had identified a South West hospital as a potential client, company information might be that their latest annual report reveals that the hospital has a big focus on improving service levels to its patients. We might also find they are under pressure to reduce administrative expenses and increase the number of beds in the main hospital facility.

- **Contact**. We can personalise based off of the **contact**. Continuing the previous example, we might find that Simon Smith, the Records Administrator, recently presented at a digital health industry conference. We learn from his presentation that he has a focus on patient record security, easy access to the records system and reducing the cost of their records administration.

- **Customers**. We can personalise based on **customer** trends and demographics. In the hospital example, we find out there is a trend towards patients wanting easy access to their health records, that they are very concerned with privacy and are also very open to eHealth solutions.

- **Competitors or Industry**. We can also customise our message with information about their **competitors** or the industry as a whole. For the hospital, this could be that there are new government guidelines for hospital records that will come into effect in six months. We might also discover that this hospital is planning to join a national network of hospitals around the country and that they will need to establish some common protocols for managing and sharing their records.

3 **Create a structured contact plan.** The contact plan should outline every touchpoint for target accounts, including the format of each touchpoint (such as email, phone, social media and so on), the messaging for each touchpoint, the follow-up, and so on. Learning how to research prospects and put effective messages together should be a core skill for your SDRs, and actually for all salespeople.

4 **Qualify your prospects.** The next step is to qualify these targets by determining who's ready to buy and who isn't. Of course it's important to continue engaging with those that are not ready to buy to keep those leads warm, but the focus should be those who are in a buying window. This helps sales teams maximise their time with key potential buyers.

Qualification is drastically different from discovery. In the discovery stage (Step 2 in this process), the goal is getting the pulse on the account. This stage is about determining who is in a buying window – who is a qualified lead, and who can be nurtured over time.

I've seen first-hand the success created with this approach so I seriously urge you to direct your prospecting efforts more in the quality direction. While the team's overall activity metrics will be lower, the activities they do perform will be far more effective. They will be cutting through the noise, reaching your ideal prospects and delivering plenty of juicy, qualified leads.

It's only once the lead-gen team can distinguish high-quality leads that the lead-gen activities discussed in this chapter will have an impact.

The art of warm calling

According to a study by the Keller Research Centre, just one per cent of cold calls ultimately convert into appointments. Buyers simply don't respond to cold calls. In fact, most buyers don't even answer calls if they don't recognise the caller. And if we think voicemail is our saving grace in this regard, we should think again. According to Vonage and eVoice, only eighteen per cent of people check voicemail from recognised numbers.

It takes a whopping *eighteen* calls to actually connect with a single buyer, according to TOPO, with a call-back rate of just one per cent. Assuming a 0.3 per cent booking rate and a twenty per cent win rate, it would take 6,264 cold calls to make four sales, according to Simple Sales Tracking. Ultimately, cold calling is not wanted by buyers and is bad for sellers. Instead, we should be warm calling.

Warm calling is when you know something about the customer before making a call. You've probably touched that customer a few times before the call – through social, through email, through them subscribing to your company's blog or newsletter, or downloading a whitepaper, and so on.

Warm calling is proven to work. In fact, according to Sales Benchmark Index, salespeople are 4.2 times more likely to gain an appointment if they already have a personal connection with the buyer.

So, how can we make our sales calls as effective as possible? Firstly, by ensuring we've done our research before making the call, as discussed earlier, so that we don't waste any time during the call itself. So rather than asking the recipient, 'How's your day going?' or 'What job do you do?' or 'What's your job title?', we should say something like this:

'[Name], I know you're the [job title] of [company]. There's a lot of change in that world, with [competitors], [industry pressures] and so on. I've spoken to people similar to you who have been able to [solve a specific problem or achieve a specific benefit] using [your company's product or service].'

This makes for a much more compelling opener. Then, once the client has registered their interest, you ask, 'Could we discuss your needs in more detail?' During that call, you extract more information from the prospect. Then you can hand that lead to the core sales function.

CREATING A STRONG VALUE NARRATIVE

According to Tony Hughes, the key to effective warm calling is to create a strong value narrative. In this Q&A, Tony explains what this is, why it's important and how to best do it.

What is a value narrative and why is it important?

It's incumbent upon us to make sure we deliver the right value narrative where we've researched the customer's industry, company and buyer persona we are targeting (the person in their role). Whether we're selling to a CFO, CEO, CIO or someone else; do we really understand what matters to them? How are they measured in their role? What are the key metrics that matter to them? Which of our other customers have moved the needle on those key metrics and are we equipped to tell these powerful true stories?

Once we've got our value narrative sorted out, we then need to atomise that message down to smaller snippets to use in a cadence of outreach via multiple channels. We need to engage through every possible business channel until we find the one that works for the prospects. This means calling, leaving a voicemail, sending a text, sending an email, connecting in LinkedIn, sending an InMail... make them know that you're determined to have a conversation. This shows them you're serious and these combinations work if you have the right narrative that's all about them and their outcomes, rather than about you and what you're selling.

Executing this requires a level of brutal personalisation. Lazy people don't do this. Winners avoid generic and instead go the extra mile in preparation and personalisation; referencing something the prospect published or wrote, a company announcement or something that's going on in their industry that's relevant.

How often should sellers engage in personalisation activity?

Every four to six working days is the right cadence. It should be a slightly different message every time, but everything needs to be all about them and not about us. You want the person looking at your messaging and thinking 'wow, this person is determined, and a conversation could be of benefit to me. They're not going to give up, I may as well reply.'

Can you provide an example of a strong value narrative?

I do a lot of work with Salesforce. They're the global leader in customer relationship management software. If I wanted to sell a CRM software system to the CEO of a medium-sized business in the financial services industry, the question I would ask myself is: 'In this industry, what really matters to them and how do they measure success?'

Let's say it's a small to medium sized business that does financial planning for clients. What are the elements of my value narrative? What of my other financial services clients achieving in terms of improved business outcomes and results? How have they driven-up the quality and volume of referrals that they're getting? Who have we managed to help reduce customer churn or improve average revenue per client? I'd be thinking about the metrics that matter to the owner of that business and then talk about results. The language of leader's is 'outcomes and managing risk, underpinned by the measurable impacts in terms of dollars, percentages and key result area (KRA) metrics'.

Then, if I was going to call I would first find a common connection I could talk with for background and support. Then I would call the prospect and say, 'hi [name]. It's Tony from Salesforce. [common connection] suggested I give you a call on the back of [attribute of their business]. I've got some ideas on how you could improve results in [specific metric they care about]. When can we find 40 minutes next week?.

Another approach might be to say you noticed an article they published on LinkedIn and that you thought they were bang on the money and that you'd like to discuss. Perhaps they just expanded to another overseas market and you could reference that as why you thought it could be right time for a conversation. They key is to reference trusted relationships and relevant trigger events.

Account-based marketing (ABM)

Like the traditional prospecting model discussed earlier, until fairly recently, marketing was also focused on generating as many leads as possible. The sales team would then have to qualify these leads and determine which ones were worth pursuing. In addition to costing a lot of money, this created significantly more work for sales teams and caused them to waste time qualifying or working on low-value leads.

With ABM, sales teams are laser-focused from the very start on the accounts we actually want, and can therefore direct valuable resources directly towards those targets. We identify the very largest and highest potential target accounts upfront, and then proactively market to those accounts. We target them very specifically, with a unique campaign for each account. While ABM used to be a labour-intensive and expensive approach only used by the biggest companies targeting the biggest accounts, advancements in technology and the proliferation of data mean that ABM can be used at scale for any business.

Here is a basic comparison between traditional B2B marketing and ABM.

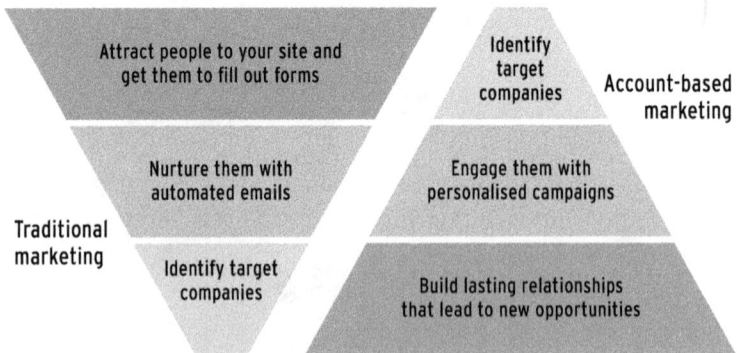

Figure 19: Traditional marketing versus ABM, Source: Drift

Instead of *ending* with a target company that's a good fit for us to sell to (after filtering out all the bad leads), ABM *starts* with target companies. The lead-gen team identifies the biggest opportunities in the market at the beginning of the process and then proactively pursues them.

According to SiriusDecisions, ninety-two per cent of B2B organisations view ABM as extremely important or very important to their marketing initiatives. And according to research from the Altera Group, ninety-seven per cent of B2B organisations said ABM had a somewhat higher or much higher return on investment than other marketing initiatives. Many studies show that companies implementing ABM have better marketing and sales alignment, better quality and faster-moving pipelines and larger deal values.

ABM very tightly aligns sales and marketing towards the same, very specific goals. Previously, there was a disconnect between sales and marketing, as sales was typically focused on specific accounts and trying to generate opportunities, while marketing usually targeted whole markets or industries.

But for us to succeed in B2B sales, we must have strong sales and marketing alignment, and ABM helps facilitate that. According to Forrester Research, companies with strong sales and marketing alignment grow at thirty-two per cent, while those without it *decline* at a rate of seven per cent.

97% of organisations that implement ABM achieve a higher ROI than with other marketing activities

If you've never done account-based marketing before, or you've tried it but didn't achieve the results you wanted, here are some key tips to get you started on the right foot:

- **Align sales and marketing**. For any ABM campaign to be a success, it is essential for the sales and marketing teams to be working together to effectively target these accounts. Without strong sales and marketing alignment, common complaints include low lead volumes, poor lead quality, poor lead follow-up and more. By achieving alignment from the beginning, both teams can achieve the results they want. It's also important to maintain alignment – sales and marketing should work together as a virtual team regardless of their reporting lines. As much as possible they should be sitting together, working together and looking at the same data, and should have the same goals and be attending the same review meetings.

- **Start with a handful of accounts**. Start by working on a joint sales and marketing plan for five or six target accounts, based on where the biggest return is likely to be, and which ones are likely to be in a buying window in the next six months. Limiting your focus gives you more resources to focus on the accounts that are most likely to convert. Once you develop a successful methodology, scale it up!

- **Tailor campaigns as much as possible**. Since you are targeting individual businesses, the campaigns should be targeted for those businesses and even the specific key stakeholders within those businesses. Create engaging content that is topical and relevant to the specific accounts and customer profiles you are targeting.

- **Engage across multiple channels**. Engage with your target contacts across various channels, since not everyone engages with the same media. This might include different social media platforms, display advertising, email, direct mail and more.

- **Define success metrics upfront**. It's essential to have clear goals and tracking in place. We not only want to achieve some lead generation or engagement metric goals, but we should be aligned that we really want solid pipeline growth, share-of-wallet improvements and actual closed deals. Course correct as needed to achieve your goals.

- **Build awareness with buyers over the long term**. Any large organisation has several stakeholders involved in any major buying decision, which means the campaign needs to reach all of those stakeholders throughout the length of the campaign. If the awareness of our company is at five per cent at the start of the campaign, the goal by the end of a three- or four-month period is for all of those stakeholders to know us intimately. Their awareness should be at ninety per cent, meaning they think of us without being prompted. That way, when they're starting to think about solutions to a particular problem, they instantly think of our company.

	Date & accounts	Messaging /content	Programs	Metrics	Team
Inception	Identifying what type of accounts and key facets for your business make sense	Identifying personas and content gaps. Do you have relevant content for all the personas?	Identification of optimal channels and programs	[Operational] Ensuring you can measure at each stage of the lifecycle. Can account activity be tracked into SFDC, or other CRM?	Identifying key players - select champion sales people
Early-stage	Joint selection of accounts between marketing and sales/customer support/ services/etc	Developing/repurposing content for key buyers so it's mostly personalised	Utilising some digital programs with other program basics	Tracking engagement (e.g. time with account) and other program metrics like CTR, inquiries, MQLAs in target accounts	Obtained stakeholder buy-in across the organisation
Mid-stage	Using predictive models and/or intent date to select accounts for additional accuracy. Identifying whether you have the contact information for the right contacts in your target accounts	Have content for all personas that's personalised and timely	Running programs that are optimised for different personas (channel, etc)	Tracking meetings with the right people in target accounts, velocity, opportunity/pipeline creation in target accounts, sales metrics	Closely in sync with your SDRs and sales team
Late-stage	Mature process of account selection and building out white space and data hygiene. Identifying ways to implement ABM for cross-sell, upsell, retention, etc	Have content for all personas that's personalised, timely and relevant	Running a combination of digital and analog programs (e.g. web personalisation and direct mail)	Hitting your KPIs. For example, revenue won in target accounts, cross-sell, upsell, renewal (stickiness)	Closely in sync with your collaborative teams and regions-SDRs, sales, support, services, etc

Figure 20: The ABM Maturity Curve, Source: Marketo

Lead scoring and management

Now we move on to lead scoring and management. Lead scoring requires businesses to rank the leads in their databases based on their sales readiness. The sales readiness of a lead is determined by analysing the prospect's current level of interest in your business.

For example, for inbound lead generation, have they visited your company website? Have they downloaded a whitepaper? Have they been to an event hosted by your company? For outbound lead generation we might look at qualifying information such as whether they are in a buying window or have identified a budget. All this activity gets sorted and scored. Lead scoring also ranks the demographics of a prospect to ensure that the prospect you are targeting actually fits into your target customer profile. This could be anything from job position to company size.

Studies show less than twenty-five per cent of acquired leads are utilised by the sales team, whereas the rest get filtered as the sales team may label them as not sales ready. Not only is this a huge loss in terms of the effort required to acquire those leads, it is a loss of leads that could have been nurtured at a later stage.

Lead scoring seeks to eliminate this by helping identify the most valuable leads, which are then passed on to the core sales team. This saves the core sales team valuable time and also increases conversion rates, thus helping the core sales team stay motivated.

Lead scoring also leads to increased marketing effectiveness. It ranks and categorises leads based on demographic and firmographic attributes, as well as behavioural attributes (in the form of clicks, website visits and so on), which helps marketing identify different categories and build different marketing strategies to target those different categories.

Another benefit is better lead response. Often, there are leads that need immediate attention. If such leads are not attended to on time, then the customer may go elsewhere. Lead scoring prioritises such leads over others, prompting the core sales team to act upon them first.

In contrast, failing to adopt lead scoring results in lost opportunities. According to a Gartner study, seventy per cent of leads are lost due to poor follow-up. A lack of lead scoring can also lead to a weaker conversion rate and lower ROI. A Kentico study found thirty-eight per cent of businesses experienced higher lead-to-opportunity conversion rates thanks to lead scoring, while a Marketing Sherpa study found those using lead scoring had a seventy-seven per cent boost in lead generation ROI over those not using it.

So, how can we ensure we're scoring and managing leads effectively? Follow these five key steps to develop an effective lead-scoring system:

1. Define your demographic criteria

These will be identified during the targeting and list-building phase of our prospecting planning or during the setting up of a specific campaign. Here are some questions to consider:

- What are the key attributes of the companies we are targeting? These include:
  - Industry classification
  - Geographic location
  - Company size
  - Company structure (centralised, decentralised, local, or subsidiary of a multinational)

- Within the target company, which department is most relevant to our product? (HR, finance, and so on.)

- Within this department, which is the key role? In other words, who would buy our product? (HR manager, vice president, chief financial officer, and so on.)

2. Define your behavioural criteria

These include criteria related to your product. Questions include:

- Are they using a specific competitive product?
- What is the potential buying power for our product category?

They also include buying potential. Questions include:

- Are they in the market for our type of product?
- Do they have the budget?
- What is our level of contact in the account?
- Have we identified buying criteria?
- Have we identified their buying process?
- Have we identified key buying personnel or groups?

3. Assign points to profile criteria

The next step is to assign criteria and a point value to each profile attribute you selected, separating our scoring between demographic criteria and behavioural criteria. We need to look at these separately as well as look at total scores. The demographic criteria don't change much, as they relate to basic company profile information, whereas the behavioural criteria are the key areas that will change and turn prospects into leads.

To see how this might work in reality, let's consider a large hotel chain that sells accommodation to medium-sized financial institutions. The role of the sales development function is to identify and develop worthwhile leads for the core sales team to qualify and close. To achieve this, the sales development function grades leads on the following criteria, which empowers them to prioritise and score leads in an objective and systematic way. These criteria would be agreed on with the core sales team so they know that any lead that comes through will be of high quality.

Demographic criteria

Lead criteria	Value	Points
Industry	Non-finance	-100
	Finance	0
Employee size	< 500	0
	500-1,999	10
	2,000-5,000	20
	5,001+	-100
Decision-making location	Offshore	0
	Local	10

Behavioural criteria

Lead criteria	Value	Points
Key contact	Identified	5
	Contacted	10
	Interacted	20
Current provider	4-star and below competitor	5
	5-star competitor	10
Buying power	< 1,000 room nights p.a.	-100
	1,000-1,999 room nights p.a.	25
	> 2,000 room nights p.a.	50
Buying readiness	Exploring market	20
	Identified buying criteria	20
	Identified buying process	20
	Identified buying committee	20

Figure 21: Lead-scoring criteria

You'll notice a few criteria are shaded and carry a value of minus 100 points. This means that if any of these criteria are met, then the lead will be invalid. For example, if the buying potential is below 1,000 room nights per annum, as shown in the table, then we won't pursue the opportunity. Or if their employee base is above 5,000, then we may need to pass it on to a different team, since our task is to manage the medium-sized accounts and not the larger accounts.

4. Set up a basic classification

The next step is to set up a basic classification, again with agreement from the core sales team. It might look something like this:

Point score	Classification	Description
<95	Non-SQL	Non-qualified lead
95-120	SQL1	Qualified lead
121+	SQL2	High-priority qualified lead

Figure 22: Lead-scoring classification

Here are a couple of worked examples of qualified leads and how they would score.

Lead example 1

Demographic criteria

Lead criteria	Value	Point
Industry	Non-finance	-100
	Finance	0
Employee size	< 500	0
	500-1,999	10
	2,000-5,000	20
	5,001+	-100
Decision-making location	Offshore	0
	Local	10
	DEMOGRAPHIC SCORE	10

Behavioural criteria

Lead criteria	Value	Points
Key contact	Identified	5
	Contacted	10
	Interacted	20
Current provider	4-star and below competitor	5
	5-star competitor	10
Buying power	< 1,000 room nights p.a.	-100
	1,000–1,999 room nights p.a.	25
	> 2,000 room nights p.a.	50
Buying readiness	Exploring market	20
	Identified buying criteria	20
	Identified buying process	20
	Identified buying committee	20
	BEHAVIOURAL SCORE	105
	TOTAL SCORE	115
	LEAD CATEGORY	SQL1

First off, we can see here that there are no red flags that immediately disqualify the lead. From a demographic standpoint, the target account meets our industry criteria and our employee size criteria. We have also identified that decision making is done offshore, which is a slight concern but not enough to disqualify the lead on its own.

From a behavioural point of view, we can see that we have identified and made contact with the key person, that our competitor is a four-star or lower hotel chain, and that they have substantial buying power, with purchases of over 2,000 room nights per year. We have also identified two of the key buying criteria.

Therefore, this lead scores at 115 points as an SQL1 (sales-qualified lead).

Lead example 2

Demographic criteria

Lead criteria	Value	Point
Industry	Non-finance	-100
	Finance	0
Employee size	< 500	0
	500-1,999	10
	2,000-5,000	20
	5,001+	-100
Decision-making location	Offshore	0
	Local	10
	DEMOGRAPHIC SCORE	30

Behavioural criteria

Lead criteria	Value	Points
Key contact	Identified	5
	Contacted	10
	Interacted	20
Current provider	4-star and below competitor	5
	5-star competitor	10
Buying power	< 1,000 room nights p.a.	-100
	1,000–1,999 room nights p.a.	25
	> 2,000 room nights p.a.	50
Buying readiness	Exploring market	20
	Identified buying criteria	20
	Identified buying process	20
	Identified buying committee	20
	BEHAVIOURAL SCORE	140
	TOTAL SCORE	170
	LEAD CATEGORY	SQL2

We can see that there are no red flags that immediately disqualify the lead. From a demographic standpoint, the target account meets our industry criteria and our employee size criteria. We have also identified that decision making is done locally – a positive aspect that makes the lead more attractive.

From a behavioural point of view, we see that we have had interaction with the key person, that our competitor is a five-star hotel chain, and that they have substantial buying power, with purchases of over 2,000 room nights per year. We have also identified three of the key buying criteria.

Therefore, this lead scores at 170 points as an SQL2 (a high-priority sales-qualified lead).

5. Track every lead

Of course, this will all be tracked in your CRM, or via Marketo or other specialised lead-tracking tools. Having everything in the system, with live updates all the time, makes it easy to track how we are progressing with leads or otherwise, so we can identify what's working or if we need to take corrective action. It also makes for seamless handover and communication between teams.

The inside scoop on inside sales

The term 'inside sales' was first applied to remote sales in the late 1980s, when it was set up as the direct opposite of 'outside sales' (a face-to-face field sales approach). For a long time, inside sales was seen as an outlier and was relegated to the sidelines of the sales department. Inside sales is now the dominant sales model for sales representatives in B2B, tech, SaaS, and a variety of B2C industries selling high-ticket items.

Put simply, inside sales refers to sales that are handled remotely. It routinely involves high-touch transactions over phone and email. But unlike a lot of telemarketers, inside sales professionals are highly skilled and knowledgeable. Thanks to advances in communications technology, inside sales reps can give presentations, conduct demonstrations and perform most of the functions traditionally handled by reps in the field.

According to a lead management study conducted by Massachusetts Institute of Technology, inside sales hiring is outpacing traditional (or outside) sales hiring by fifteen to one.

Why?

First, inside sales has significantly lower operational costs than outside sales, as it eliminates travelling expenses. According to *Harvard Business Review*, it costs forty to ninety per cent less to bring in new customers using inside rather than outside sales teams.

Second, buyers are becoming increasingly comfortable making purchases remotely. Many wouldn't dream of investing in a product or service without first researching it online, and would prefer a quick phone call to a formal face-to-face meeting. According to Sales Benchmark Index, seventy per cent of customers don't want an in-person meeting at all. As a result, it makes sense to have inside sales reps ready to engage with customers on their terms.

Third, with the advances in digital technologies such as videoconferencing, webinars and CRM systems, inside sales reps are increasingly able to build the same level of customer rapport as traditional sales reps – but at a fraction of the cost.

With the right sales acceleration tools, inside sales can also enhance productivity. Every year, new sales acceleration tools go to market. By forming a powerful sales technology stack (more on this in the next section), inside sales teams can gain the ability to send more emails, dial more leads and have more conversations. In fact, a study from The Bridge Group found a distinct correlation between the number of conversations that reps have a day and quota attainment.

So, what are the key points to remember with regard to inside sales? Jonathan Hunt, senior vice president of sales development at Salesforce, has identified six things we should prioritise.

1. Develop talent

An inside sales rep shouldn't stay an inside sales rep forever. On the contrary, we want them to start moving up in their career within a year. Ultimately, this benefits the business as reps continue to move forward in new sales roles, armed with new skills.

2. Focus on speed-to-lead and high-quality activities

One of the key metrics we should be managing is speed-to-lead. In other words, how fast we are calling people once a lead comes in. According to Salesforce data, if we don't call someone in the first hour, this multiplies the conversion rate drop-off by about ten times.

At the same time, we should be focusing on high-quality activity levels. We do this by setting clear targets and ensuring the team is able to successfully meet them on a daily basis. Any shortfall in activity will have a material impact on our annualised contract value, or ACV (the average annualised revenue per customer contract).

3. Set up inside sales reps for success

All inside sales reps must undergo training. As an example, at Salesforce, new inside sales reps must complete intensive training via the company's education management system, Trailhead, which includes simulations, product and sales skills education, call shadowing, and stand-and-deliver presentations.

This should be followed by in-person training, where we train and test across our sales process and product offerings. As sales leaders, we should spend several hours a week with all reps, listening to their calls with our telephony tools and coaching them live.

4. Provide incentives and support healthy competition

Motivating inside sales reps is crucial, and the biggest motivator for reps is being promoted to Account Executive. At Salesforce, sales development reps know that by the end of twelve months, they will have the opportunity for a promotion. However, they only receive a promotion if their metrics and stack rankings are above required levels.

On top of that, we can support healthy competition by posting results every day on an internal communication platform, calling out the top performers, offering competitive challenges, and sharing staff rankings.

5. Be persistent

Connecting with a lead requires persistence. It can take as many as five attempts, and sometimes more, to connect. So, with that in mind, try and put five touches on a lead (either a call, email or both) over the course of ten days to two weeks. Then, after a fifth and final attempt to reach a lead, let it go.

Of course, the goal is not to reach the fifth touch before successfully connecting, but to connect as early as possible. Because the more time we spend on one customer, the less capacity we have for other potential leads.

6. Partner closely with marketing

It's important for inside sales reps to develop a close partnership with the marketing team. Marketing is often eager to do training for inside sales reps, and since inside sales reps are increasingly on the frontline, it's critical for them to have the latest information on the company's products or services. We should also encourage marketing to listen in on customer calls to get more insight into customers' thoughts and preferences.

Building a powerful sales technology stack

Sales technology will play an increasingly important role in the new sales landscape, so it's important for sales teams to adopt the right mindset. Victor Antonio, the sales keynote speaker I mentioned in Part 1, is excited about what the future holds for sales tech, and its impact on the sales profession. He gives the example of a large healthcare company he worked with recently.

'They walked me into their call centre, where a hundred or so people were making calls. Let's say each person makes a hundred calls per day. That's 10,000 calls. But let's say only twenty per cent of those calls close. What do you do with the other eighty per cent? Who do you follow up with? It's a big question,' he says.

'To help answer it, this company was using artificial intelligence – machine learning – to analyse the audio between the caller and the recipient. It analysed the audio based on the words used, velocity, intonation and so on. Based on this, it could tell if the customer was likely to buy or not. This helped the salesperson better prioritise leads.

'It also improved coaching and training, because it could tell if the salesperson missed something. If a competitor was mentioned, for example, did the salesperson say the right things to block that objection? So the company was using natural language processing to determine who's more likely to buy and whether the salesperson needs to be trained more, and on what topics specifically.'

Antonio says rather than fearing technology such as AI, sales teams should embrace it.

'When it comes to AI, the most pressing question is, "Will it replace the average salesperson?" The answer is no, and that's the wrong way of looking at it,' he says.

'As a salesperson, think about every step you have to take, and every activity you have to perform, to do your job. Artificial intelligence is going to take over tasks that are mundane or routine, so you have more time to sell. It's going to augment our ability to sell more effectively. Much like the healthcare company that was able to analyse sales calls and then prioritise them, that removes that burden from the salesperson.'

Victor says the beauty of AI is that it's completely objective. This is in stark contrast to salespeople, who tend to have 'happy ears'.

'Salespeople hear what they want to hear. But a machine is very objective – it'll hear what it needs to hear to make a decision. More and more, we're going to be working through a CRM – whether it's Salesforce, Microsoft, Zoho, or something else. This CRM is now going to become a platform of acceleration. This is where everything is going to happen – from sales calls and video conferences to emails and text messages.

'So, your CRM system will be able to capture all those seller-buyer interactions, whether it's a text, whether it's a posting on social media, whether it's an email, and so on. It's going to be able to analyse all that information, and give you much more data and insight into the customer than you have today. That is the power of where this is going. That's the power of using AI.'

Victor cites Salesforce's Einstein product as an example. Built into the Salesforce platform, Einstein is a layer of artificial intelligence that delivers predictions and recommendations based on each client's unique business processes and customer data. Clients can then use those insights to automate responses and actions, boosting employee productivity and customer satisfaction.

'Salesforce's Einstein product is just amazing. Whenever we give a price or a quote to a potential customer, the big question is, "What level of discounts should we be giving?" Obviously, the answer should be zero, but there's always a discount if you want to be competitive,' says Victor.

'So, the system will analyse conversations, past wins and past losses, and actually suggest what discount rate you should give in a particular quote to make you more likely to win the deal rather than not. Then, it will provide you with some insight as to why.'

As sales acceleration technology continues to grow more powerful, sales teams will get better at knowing who to sell to, what to sell them and how to sell it. If you haven't already begun outfitting your sales team with a powerful sales technology stack, it's definitely time to begin.

ARM YOUR SALES TEAMS WITH
THESE TECHNOLOGY TOOLS

Here's Jordan again with his thoughts on the tech stack required to support sales teams.

What are some of the best pieces of tech that sales leaders should consider for their teams?

In order to answer that question, let's quickly run through the sales funnel from top to bottom. At the very top you've got your pre-prospecting, which is list building and contact building. Then, as we move down the funnel, we start actually reaching out. That's when you have your actual outbound prospecting.

Then you book a meeting. You conduct the meeting through something like Zoom. You run the discovery and qualification. After that is generally some sort of presentation demo, followed by negotiation and closing.

There are solutions at each point of that journey that add value. So, when we think about pre-prospecting – building account lists and building lead lists – that's a very low-value activity for an Account Executive, or a business development manager, to be putting their time towards. There are solutions such as:

ZoomInfo: ZoomInfo helps you find the prospects you're looking for based on industry, location, company size, company revenue, job title, job function and more. ZoomInfo's database provides access to more direct dials and email addresses than any other market intelligence provider.

DiscoverOrg: Designed to reduce the time-to-direct-connection with targeted prospects, the DiscoverOrg platform improves the performance of all prospecting efforts by providing both the contacts and context needed to sell and market more effectively.

What about outbound prospecting? Which tech tools are helpful here?

If I'm doing nine touches, then there are going to be days when I'm doing my fifth touch on some accounts, my seventh touch on other accounts, and my third touch on other accounts. That's extremely difficult to manage. Some of the solutions that come to mind on that front, and that I see a lot of people utilising, are:

SalesLoft: Though its original product offering focused on sales development, SalesLoft has expanded its platform to offer increased functionality for the entire sales team, including personalised communication and cloud-based sales engagement.

Reach: Reach's goal is to influence buyers at each stage of their buying journey. It does this by taking big data sources and turning them into relevant, actionable insights for each client's geographies, markets and categories.

Mixmax: Mixmax accelerates productivity, so sales reps can reach more prospects, land more meetings and close more deals. Features include scheduling messages to send later, sending personalised emails at scale, and logging emails, opens, clicks and downloads to your CRM.

Are there any other tech tools we should prioritise?

Yes, in the discovery and qualification area. This is the area that I think many organisations don't realise how much they may be struggling in. It's the questions that the reps are asking, and how they're navigating those calls.

There's this amazing set of solutions that are coming out right now that are really, truly built and backed through machine learning and artificial intelligence, including:

Gong: Gong offers conversation intelligence technology specifically for sales teams. It captures all of your sales conversations – including customer calls, web conferences and emails – and uses AI to help you see how deals are progressing and what you could be doing better.

What are the benefits of using technology like Gong?

It's all centred around conversation analysis. So, being able to have a bot listen to the whole sales call, dissect what the seller is saying, and offer the salesperson some insight into that conversation, and also to the leaders who are managing the sales team.

So, rather than having to listen in on 100 sales calls, they're going to be able to pull out all the key pieces of information and tidbits. Like any time that pricing is mentioned, or any time the word 'discount' is mentioned. Then the sales leader can say, 'What did my seller say when that specific objection came up? How did we handle it? Oh, we didn't handle it that great. Let's work through that in a coaching session.'

So, the sales tech on that front – discovery and qualification – is the area that I believe can have the biggest impact on sales organisations right now.

SUMMARY

That brings us to the end of Step 3. Before we move on to Step 4, here's a list of the key points to remember:

- There are four main sources of prospects in the context of B2B sales: outbound lead activity, inbound lead activity, prospecting activity, and referrals from existing customers.

- Focusing only on quantity metrics with big volumes of customer contact across the market doesn't work. We must focus on quality activities.

- We need to focus on the highest priority potential accounts and highly customise our approach to each prospect. In order to do this effectively, we need to do our research and create a strong value narrative.

- With account-based marketing, instead of *ending* with a target company that's a good fit for us to sell to, we *start* with target companies. We identify the biggest opportunities at the beginning and then proactively pursue them.

- Lead scoring helps us determine the sales readiness of our prospects. To develop an effective lead-scoring system, we need to define our demographic and behavioural criteria, assign points to profile criteria, set up a basic classification and track every lead.

- Inside sales is now the dominant sales model for sales representatives in B2B, tech, SaaS, and a variety of B2C industries selling high-ticket items.

- Sales technology will become increasingly important in the new sales landscape. If you haven't already begun outfitting your sales team with a powerful sales technology stack, it's time to begin.

Step 4: Build High-Converting Middle-of-the-Funnel (MOFU) Capability

'Excellence is an art won by training and habituation...
Excellence then is not an act but a habit.'

ARISTOTLE

In the past, the traditional salesperson managed the entire sales funnel – from prospecting to conversion to after-sales customer care. But, as we've covered, the future-proof sales structure is built around specialised and well-equipped teams designed to handle specific sales activities. The Customer Success team will proactively manage the day-to-day account management of existing accounts, so we no longer need our expensive sales resource tied up with these routine tasks. There will also be a dedicated Prospecting and Lead Generation function, meaning another big responsibility has moved off the traditional field sales team's plate.

Ultimately, the traditional field salesperson no longer owns the entire funnel – which means they will need to focus on MOFU to deliver the most value and the highest business return.

The problem is that many so-called 'professional' salespeople are not professional at all. They have learnt on the job or from their managers, they often aren't aware of the key trends shaping the sales profession, and are not actively improving their skills. According to Gallup, only twenty-six per cent of sales representatives are actively engaged in their job. Fifty-five per cent are not engaged and nineteen per cent are actively disengaged.

But MOFU is where the rubber hits the road, so to speak. Companies make huge investments in their products, their services, their facilities and their staff, so it is critical that when a potential or existing customer meets your salesperson, it is a high-quality and professional interaction – one where the customer feels they're getting value right from the start. Our salespeople must be capable of establishing credibility by bringing value to customers from the first meeting.

By contrast, when an unprofessional, underequipped salesperson comes up against the modern, well-informed buyer, they won't get far. Even deals they do win will most likely be plagued by delays, as objections that weren't uncovered and addressed earlier rear their ugly heads. Then, in a desperate bid to bring business forward, they are more likely to offer huge incentives and discounts, or miss their targets.

To avoid these risks, we need to ensure our core salespeople are highly competent and professional in MOFU activities. Can they take customers through this complex journey? Can they deliver value from the first meeting? Can they build credibility? Can they build the trust to gain cooperation on building business cases? Can they uncover the buying process and get access to the change agents and key decision makers?

To master these skills, core salespeople will need to become expert in the areas of qualifying and questioning, insight selling, storytelling, and negotiation and deal management.

Qualifying and questioning

Qualifying refers to the process of determining if a prospect has certain characteristics (such as ability, authority and inclination to purchase) that qualify them as an ideal customer. While effective qualifying is critical to sales success, so few salespeople and sales organisations are effective qualifiers.

This has so many negative implications, the most serious of which is that salespeople work on unqualified opportunities, which burns through time that could be spent on opportunities that are qualified and, therefore, have a higher chance of closing.

It is costly to commit sales time and company resources to large deals, so we need to direct these precious resources to the best opportunities. And this isn't just at the beginning of the sales process – we need to be qualifying throughout the whole sales process. According to Michele Buckley at Gartner, qualifying needs to happen continuously, rather than as a one-off activity – particularly as the buying process becomes increasingly complex.

'With every sales interaction, you need to regularly check in with what's known and what's unknown. We call this continuous qualification,' she says.

'Do not assume that the stakeholders you were introduced to at the beginning of the sales cycle will be the same midway through the sales cycle, or later. Do not assume that the approvers that you've identified will remain the same. Don't assume that the requirements will remain the same throughout the opportunity.

'Don't assume that the timeframe is accurate, either. We're finding – due to all this complexity – that buyers actually don't know how long it's going to take to make a purchase. They don't do it that often. We've seen data points that say it actually takes them ninety-seven per cent longer to make a purchase than they anticipated. So, don't assume whatever the client says is factual. They might think it's September but, in fact, it may be the following April. This is not done out of malicious intent. They actually just don't know.

'So, sales leaders need to encourage their teams to continually qualify opportunities. Meaning, ask questions and check to make sure that the facts they have are still correct. That the information they provided is still relevant. That every aspect of the sales deal serves to validate all those data points they collect.'

KEY INSIGHTS INTO EFFECTIVE QUALIFYING

In Step 3, Jordan Mara shared his thoughts on building a powerful sales technology stack to support sales teams. Here, Jordan shares his thoughts on qualifying.

You encourage sales teams to look at specific customer outcomes or customer actions as their key metrics, rather than high-level activity metrics. What does that look like?

Nobody should be reaching out to a prospect that's outside of their ideal customer profile. Before even doing any outbound prospecting, we should first be asking, 'Who are our customers? Who are we adding value to? Who is renewing with us?' From there, once you have that ideal customer profile built out, it's then a matter of going about prospecting them in a systematic manner, where there's a much larger focus on the quality side.

If you work back from the revenue number that you have to close, it probably won't end up being some astronomical number of sales. It's going to be a much lower number of accounts that you actually have to sell to. The key there is to be getting into those very specific accounts, which you know you can add tons and tons of value to.

The first step on that journey is a conversation. We have to have two-way connection, and the prospect agreeing that, 'Yes. We would like to learn more about what this message is that we've received from you, or what this call was that we got from you.' It's at that point that you can then begin to make a bit of a plan as to how to win that account.

The metric that I'm always most focused on and most interested in is the number of initial meetings, initial appointments or initial discoveries that an Account Executive, an SDR or a business development manager has over the course of a quarter.

What qualifies as a discovery or this metric that you're talking about?

One thing that I'm quite ruthless on is qualification. From a sales perspective, people are very rarely in a sales motion. So, if we are trying to sell to them when they're not looking to buy, then it creates this imbalance, or a misalignment, between the conversations that you're having. That just gets uncomfortable.

So, qualification is drastically different than discovery. In that discovery piece, I'm really just interested in getting the pulse on the account. If only ten or twenty per cent of those accounts that we talk to are in a buying motion, that's totally fine because we've had the ten or the 100 conversations. Now, what do we do with the remaining eighty per cent that aren't in a buying motion, but are the right buyers – the right individuals – that we need to now nurture over a longer period of time?

How do we narrow that target universe to begin with? What sort of process do we go through?

So, one way to look at this is essentially three layers of qualification. First, we need to qualify the account. Is this a business that will get value from our offering? Then, we need to qualify the prospect or the individual that we're talking to. Is this the person that will be able to buy our solution, at a company that will get value from our solution? Then we need to qualify the opportunity. Is the problem that they have, the challenge they have, or the opportunity that they're looking to capitalise on, in line with the value that our solution can bring to the table?

So, if we start by looking at all the accounts out there and we narrow them down to a specific segment of the market, we're left with an account list that we can go after. Then, it's all about finding that right set of individuals who would make up the buyer personas. Then, from there into, essentially, what the use cases and business impacts are.

How can we use specific targeting to break through all the noise?

What I encourage all of my customers to do is follow what I call the four Cs. When we think about an account and the prospects at that account, we can personalise our communication based off of one of four Cs:

- We can personalise based off of the **contact**. So, the specific individual that we're reaching out to.

- We can personalise it based off something about the **company**. So, whether it was something that they put up on their website. Something that they shared on social. Something in the news. Something about that company.

- We can personalise based off of their **customer**, and what we know about their customer. Key insights that we have there.

- Or we can customise and personalise our message to this account, or this prospect, based off of their **competitors** or the industry as a whole.

So, what this allows a seller to do is make sense of all that noise that's out there. Rather than running around trying to think, 'Okay. Do I pull a piece of information here? Do I pull a piece of information there? What's good? What's bad?', I just need one tidbit on the contact. One tidbit on the company. One nugget on the customer of theirs. Then, something on the competitor or the industry as a whole. Now, you've got a plethora of really great, meaningful information to use and to weave into your reach-outs to those accounts.

With regard to questioning, the key is not talking about ourselves, our products and our companies too much, especially in the early part of the sales process. What we're trying to do – with our knowledge of the customer's business, their industry and their competitors, and with our knowledge of our products – is build a business case for the customer to change. We want to move the customer from A, their current status quo, to B, a much better scenario that includes our solution.

For example, if a salesperson approached the Commonwealth Bank with the goal of selling ATM security software and the bank admitted they were worried about money laundering and needed a security solution, the typical response would be, 'Here's what we can do. Here's what we did for other banks. It's going to cost this much. Let me give you a demonstration.'

Rather than jumping into a pitch at the first opportunity, the qualifying and questioning approach turns the discussion back to the customer. In this approach, the salesperson would say something like, 'Yes, we've developed solutions for this problem before. How would you implement something like that in the bank? What are the main issues with your current software?' This encourages the customer to think more deeply about their problem instead of evaluating the proposed solution.

It's quite a job converting salespeople to this questioning method, because they're just bursting to jump to the end where they present the solution. This is because, traditionally, the marketing and product teams have filled their heads with all the features and benefits of their products – how they work and how good they are. This means most salespeople are very good at talking about 'B' – what the world will look like if the customer implements the solution.

Questioning really helps sales teams get at the customer's 'A' – their current status quo – and build the business case for change. Salespeople should be like surgeons with scalpels – slicing into the customer's problem and magnifying it – to make the customer realise they've got to change.

Going back to the Commonwealth Bank example, further questions might include, 'How would you make a purchase like this? Who would be involved?' The goal here is getting the customer to describe the problem – and ideal solution – in their own words. We should be questioning the customer thoroughly before even touching on potential solutions.

A key phrase to remember here is, 'Slow down to sell faster.' Really take the time to understand the customer's business. Engage authentically and with real curiosity. Understand what they need, why they need it and when they need it. By doing so, you'll sell fast; your sales cycle will be shortened.

An insight into insight selling

The sales profession is no longer just about building relationships. That's not to say relationships no longer matter in B2B sales. Rather, what the data tells us is that it's the nature of the relationships that matters.

In our conversations with potential buyers, we need to provide value for them, rather than adopting a friending strategy. According to Tony Hughes, 'Nobody worth selling to – if they're a senior person – is lonely, bored and looking for a friend. None of them are lying awake at night, hoping some sales rep will call them tomorrow and give them a sales pitch.' Our target customers are busy and stressed. So we've got to find a way to get through to them. We can do this by delivering insights; this is known as insight selling.

Insights are accurate understandings of a person or thing. In sales, they're gathered through research, experience and data, and used to forge a deeper relationship with a prospective client. Insight selling is the art of using insights to move the deal forward by speaking directly to prospect needs in a way that traditional sales techniques cannot. Through insight we challenge the status quo in the customer's business and build the case for making a change.

'Buyers want to talk to sellers, but only if they bring some value to the table' – INSIGHT SELLING

Insight selling is often plotted on a continuum of sales evolution – product selling to solution selling to insight selling. And it is true that insight selling sits at the top of the sales hierarchy today as far as sales methods are concerned, but it is absolutely not a new thing. In fact, the fundamentals of insight selling have been in force for the past 130 years.

In 1887, John Henry Patterson, the founder of the National Cash Register Company (NCR) and a pioneer of modern selling, made sales effectiveness a top priority for his company. He laid out an extensive sales and sales management system that included the concept of building trust with the buyer and understanding their business before talking about the product. He even had his salespeople study accounting to better understand the small businesses they sold to.

This was an early example of insight selling – he had his salespeople understand the problems that small businesses face to create demand for his cash registers. Thomas J. Watson's blue-suited army of IBM sales professionals hardly talked about their products and solutions, they talked to CEOs and other senior executives about the potential for transforming their businesses and growing into new markets. Since then, all good salespeople have used insight selling even if they didn't call it that or know they were doing it.

More recently, the books *Insight Selling* and *The Challenger Sale*, along with several other sales studies, have brought the role of insight selling in the modern market to the fore.

When it comes to the practical application of insight selling, the core process is outlined in Figure 24.

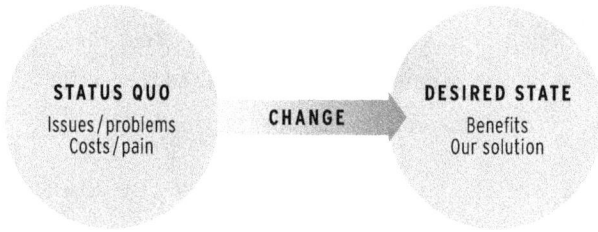

- Seller identifies and aligns with the **CHANGE AGENTS** in the account.
- Seller helps the customer understand the **PAIN** of staying with the status quo.
- Seller helps the customer understand the benefits of the change.
- Seller helps the customer with their buying process, navigate Buying Committee.

Figure 24: Insight selling

Here's an example of insight selling in action:

'[Buyer's name], we're seeing some troubling trends in the market with [brief issue summary], which is leading to [impacts]. Is this an issue you're experiencing yet or looking to avoid at [company name]?

'This is surprising to some, but we have some data that shows [share insight]. Based on that, and what we've learnt from our experience with our clients, we're now suggesting [solution]. We've had great success with this. In fact, with [company name], we even [cite major outcome], which we've built a case study around.'

One big benefit of insight selling is avoiding a 'no decision' outcome. When I ask most sales teams about their biggest enemy, they assume it's their competitors. The truth is that our biggest enemy isn't other competitors – it's 'no decision', or no change from the status quo. This is becoming more of a problem because buying decisions are more complex and involve more people, and are therefore harder to make. So, if the customer's current solution is working okay, or they can put a Band-Aid solution on the problem, they won't consider other solutions.

As B2B sellers, we're very good at selling against the competition. Namely, by getting the customer to understand that we have the best solution. But that's just not enough to close deals these days.

Customers will often say, 'You've got the best solution, but we've decided not to do anything.' This is the dreaded 'no decision', or a decision to stay with the status quo. This means we've done a good job selling the benefits of our solution, but haven't spent enough time building the case for change.

Insight selling helps us avoid that by prompting us to work with the customer, very actively, on what their status quo is and what the cost of that is to them. They may be doing things a certain way, and it's not optimal, but do they recognise that? Can they associate a cost with that? Insight selling helps the customer recognise problems and act on them.

In contrast, solution selling – which is how the majority of sales reps sell – is based on the concept of asking big, open-ended questions to understand customer needs before crafting a potential solution. This includes questions like, 'What are your top three priorities for the year?' and 'What are the biggest challenges you're facing right now, and how did they arise?'

Solution selling rose to popularity in the 1980s and still enjoys widespread adoption today. However, it's becoming less effective due to oversaturation and information overload, with too many reps using this approach and buyers' easy access to product information. In short, if we continue to sell this way, we'll fail to stand out or, worse, contribute to customers' sense of overwhelm.

It's worth pointing out that open-ended questions aren't wrong – they're simply inefficient for the modern buyer and don't create unique value. So, instead of waiting to tie our solution to something our prospect said, we can lead with, 'Most business leaders like you that I speak to are worried about [issue one, issue two, issue three]. And the best companies I speak with are doing [X, Y and Z]. How are you approaching this challenge?'

As sales leaders, we need to equip our sellers to move away from conversations that start with, 'This is who I am. This is my company. This is what we do, and here's how it works.' No one's interested in that if they're not yet a customer. If you work for Salesforce, for example, you shouldn't be opening with, 'Hey [name]. I'm with Salesforce. We're the global leader in customer success software.' Even though that's true, the customer doesn't care about us being the global leader, until they first understand why a conversation with us could be a benefit to them.

Given this, we need to ensure that every engagement is all about the customer rather than ourselves. This means asking, 'How do I provide value for the potential buyer, well in advance of them deriving value as a customer?' In other words, what insights can I offer the customer? What fresh point of view can I offer the people I'm seeking conversations with?

AN EIGHT-STEP INSIGHT SELLING FRAMEWORK

Brian Signorelli, director of HubSpot's Global Sales Partner Program, has outlined an eight-step insight selling framework you can use when engaging with potential customers:

- 'The current state of the world is [mega-trends one, two and three].'

- '[Mega-trend] makes life challenging for business leaders like you because [implication one, two and three] ...'

- '... and this is only going to get harder in the future because [reasons one, two and three].'

- 'Today, the way most companies try to solve [challenge or mega-trend] is [hire more people, spend more money, and so on].'

- 'The outcome for most companies is [mediocre results].'

- 'But there's a small group of [companies or business leaders] doing things differently ...'

- '... and these are the results they're getting [should be far better than what the middle-of-the-road company is getting in slide number five].'

- 'Here's how it works [this is where we discuss our company's service or product].'

Remember, we live in the age of information and the empowered buyer. Everything our prospect wants to know about us, our company, and our products and services is available online. If we can't bring unique value to the customer, they have no reason to speak with us.

So, how do we generate insights? Victor Antonio believes marketing has a major role to play here.

'As a salesperson, I should be focused on selling activities. I don't want to spend my time researching. So, if marketing can help us generate those insights, great,' he says.

'Marketing can review case studies, look at recent research being done within the market, and monitor the changes in the environment – regulations, policies, whatever it may be. Maybe through that, they can give the salesperson some insight. Like, "Mention this to your customer. Raise this objection. Raise this point with your customer."

'If marketing can't help us, we as salespeople have to generate our own insights. How do we do that? Visualise a Venn diagram. The ideal salesperson should understand their products or services, but also understand the customer's needs. Where are they missing something? What are they not seeing?

'This requires me to understand their business, my products and services, and what's going on in the market. There is no shortcut to that. You've got to read. You've got to marinate. Then, you should be able to see slants in the market. By slants, I mean new angles that you can approach the customer from. The customer will then say, "Wow. I never thought about it that way." That's what you want.'

I agree totally with Victor's direction here and I actually use the following Venn diagram when I am explaining insight and the unique insight each of us is capable of. We just need to apply what we know from other customers, what we know about our products and company, and what we know from our own experience and industry knowledge. Then combine it into something meaningful that applies to your current customer's situation, ideally using a story.

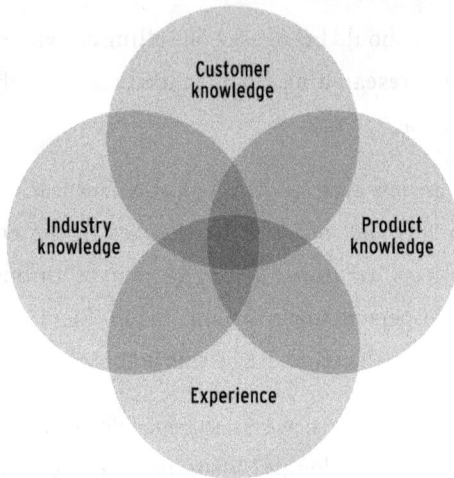

Figure 25: Insight comes from intersections

The power of storytelling

From time immemorial humans have related to stories, and it is no different in the sales world. Storytelling has long been a secret and powerful weapon of the best salespeople. According to Jennifer Aeker at Stanford University, we are twenty-two times more likely to remember stories than facts alone. Think about the compelling presentations you've seen – was it the facts and figures that resonated with you, or was it the story behind them?

Effective storytelling interacts with the brain very differently from when we are sharing facts and figures. According to molecular biologist and the author of *Brain Rules* John Medina, 'When the brain detects an emotionally charged event, the amygdala releases dopamine into the system. Because dopamine greatly aids memory and information processing, you could say it creates a Post-it note that reads, "Remember this."'

Why does this happen? Author of *Mirroring People*, Marco Lacoboni, explains that it comes down to mirror neurons – brain cells that recreate experiences based on what we are interacting with. This can be as simple as returning a smile, but when it comes to storytelling, it means that our brains recreate the stories to the extent that we experience the events ourselves. This is why stories are far more engaging and memorable than facts.

How is this relevant to selling?

If facts are not engaging or memorable, salespeople can no longer rely on sales conversations that focus on product specifications, and lists of features and benefits. To engage the customer and stand out from the competition, they need to tell stories.

In sales, stories can be used to break the ice, build rapport, illustrate the benefits of the solution and more. The challenge is that most salespeople don't tell stories – they struggle to find the right story in the moment, or don't know how to make a story compelling or relevant to the customer.

Fortunately, this is an area where a lot of information has been published, including Mike Adams's book *Seven Stories Every Salesperson Must Tell*. Mike also has some great content on YouTube that I recommend.

When creating stories (which core salespeople should be doing in advance of any sales meeting), Mike suggests that the following five elements should be present:

1   **A central character.** This is the hero of the story – the protagonist. Keep in mind that, when it comes to choosing your stories, effective sales stories are *not* case studies and they are not stories about how good an individual salesperson or the company is. Stories with the

salesperson or company as the central character immediately turn customers off. Instead, the hero of our stories has to be a customer, or a person or company that the potential customer can relate to.

2   **A sequence of events.** The sequence of events is the challenge experienced by the central character, the initiative they took to solve it and the benefits they reaped as a result. Yes, our company or products can have a presence in this story and it is at least implied that we were a key enabler, but this is not the central point. The point is the hero's journey, not the successful sale.

3   **A story framework.** The framework is how the events are organised in order to make a compelling story. Rather than just listing event after event, a story needs to establish setting, share a surprising complication and how this affected the central character, describe the moment at which events turned in the character's favour (or out of their favour, depending on whether it is a positive or negative story), and present the resolution.

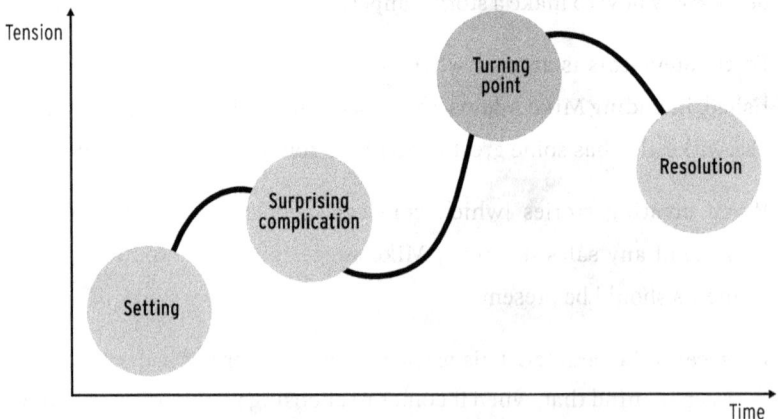

Figure 26: Storytelling structure

4   **An unpredictable surprise.** The unpredictable surprise is one of the stages in the aforementioned framework – something that will catch the audience's attention because they aren't expecting it. This also triggers the brain to try to figure out what will happen next, or how the problem will be solved, thereby ensuring that you have their attention.

5   **A business point or relevant insight.** When we tell these types of stories, we boost our own credibility by demonstrating our knowledge of the listener's industry and the challenges in it. We are edging towards discussing their business and their challenges in a non-confrontational way. Taking this approach can quickly lower the barriers to meaningful and insightful discussions.

Mike shares the following company culture story as an example. 'One of the most famous tech companies in the world is HP. It was founded in 1938 in California, and in the early days of the company Bill Hewlett, one of the founders, went into work on the weekend and found that the tool room with all the equipment in it was locked. So he took a fire-axe and smashed the door open. He left a note on the door which said, "This door will never be locked again because we trust our people".' This story ticks all the boxes for a proper sales story.

I implore you to make storytelling a key weapon in your sales arsenal. It should be pervasive throughout the selling process and it's a great way to bring insight into the discussion. Dig out the great stories among your team, craft them into an effective structure and actively share them with your whole sales group. At your team meetings I suggest that you always share stories and practise storytelling.

Negotiation and deal management

As stated earlier, it's absolutely crucial for the core sales team to have a high level of professionalism in the areas of negotiation and deal management. The comparative quality and profitability of the deals our salespeople generate is the true measure of their value to the company.

At present, there's too much poor selling going on, where the salesperson comes back to management and says, 'Yeah, I got the deal, but we're going to have to discount twenty-five per cent.' Often management is put in the difficult position where they have to accept these terms since they want the business, and it's too late in the game to go back with a counter offer. Compare this to the salesperson who says, 'Okay. I can get us this deal. I'm going to give a ten per cent discount, but in exchange we're going to get a three-year term. And the customer has agreed to a clause for out-of-scope services that should net us an extra $50,000 a month.'

In any B2B organisation, results will increase exponentially by encouraging the behaviours of the second salesperson while eliminating the behaviours of the first.

How can sales leaders encourage the behaviours of the second salesperson throughout their team?

Effective prospecting processes and following the sales techniques discussed so far in this step will go a long way to setting the stage for a seamless close. However, there will still be occasions when salespeople will be faced with a serious negotiation and will find themselves having to deal with a professional procurement or contracts team towards the end of the sales cycle. The key to managing this process is preparation.

First off, when we think about negotiating with professional buyers we need to consider how they are thinking about the situation. Professional buyers are trained to simplify deals as much as possible so that they can narrow the focus towards a price discussion. Many are also paid based on how much they can *save* their company, which means it's in their best interest to negotiate your prices down. Consequently, they will attempt to commoditise the solution and bring everything down to a price discussion.

This therefore means the role of a sales team is to complexify the deal as much as possible with inclusions and other offers, as well as terms and conditions. This will prevent the company and solution from being seen as a commodity, and also creates more levers with which the team can negotiate. Take the example I shared earlier – the salesperson gave a discount but in return got a long-term commitment from the customer and the insertion of an out-of-scope clause. The other salesperson just gave the farm away and discounted the product heavily.

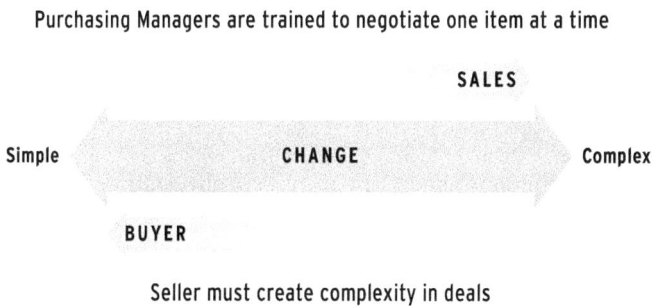

Purchasing Managers are trained to negotiate one item at a time

SALES

Simple   CHANGE   Complex

BUYER

Seller must create complexity in deals

Figure 27: Deal complexity, Source: Growth Acumen

Let me run you through a real-life example of a negotiation. I was engaged by a large IT vendor to help them in their negotiations with major distributors and resellers. They hadn't been achieving great outcomes, with sales discussions often getting stuck in a tug-of-war around discount levels and the volume commitment. Of course, the vendor didn't want to give much of a discount without a big commitment and the distributors and resellers wanted a big discount but were cautious on the volume commitment.

This vendor wanted to improve their approach and outcomes and, with another big negotiation looming on the horizon, they had to move fast. We worked towards that deal with a strategy of expanding the list of negotiable items beyond discounts and volume commitments. The team brainstormed what those items could be and got clear on the acceptable outcomes for each of the items and what the initial offer would be. If possible, vendor businesses should always be the ones making the offer or proposal, as this creates scope to frame the discussion and terms, so teach your MOFU sales teams to focus on this goal throughout the sales process. We want to avoid having to respond to the customer's contract and terms.

Here is the list of negotiable items and ranges, from the vendor's point of view. Can you see how adding complexity in this way makes it easier to reach a compromise and ultimately close the deal?

Item	Acceptable range	Initial offer(from vendor)
Annual sales commitment	$5-7 million	$7 million
Discount from list price	30-35%	30%
Marketing funding from vendor	3-5%	2.5%
Portion of 'high-value' products	15-25%	25%
Personnel commitment from vendor	1-2 headcount	1 headcount
Level of quarterly rebate	2-3%	2%
Exclusivity or not by channel	Exclusive in some channels	Non-exclusive
Term of agreement	2-3 years	1 year
Termination terms	30-90 days' notice	30 days
Right of return for slow-moving stock	Up to 2% stock rotation	No returns
Payment terms	30-60 days	30 days
Service commitments	Up to 0.5% refund support	No support

Figure 28: Negotiable items and ranges (from a vendor's point of view)

Once this list was established, when the customer asked for something beyond the initial offer we could trade off with an item elsewhere on the list. Say, for example, that they really wanted additional vendor personnel. We could then offer them an extra person in return for reducing the level of marketing support. This is the crux of creating value in negotiations – different items have different value to the buyer and seller, so trading them off creates a better deal for everyone.

This process also encourages regular deal reviews among the team, which are an excellent way to ensure we stay on track and don't get surprises late in the deal cycle. It's good to create a standard deal review template and review deals as a group. This should be separate from forecast reviews and should be conducted in a constructive and positive way. The idea is to have everyone look at the status of all of our key deals in such a meeting and give suggestions and inputs on how we can improve our chances. It's amazing the number of good ideas and amount of practical sharing that can flow in these sessions.

The other important point to make here is that closing a deal starts at the *beginning* of the deal, not at the end. Sales leaders often tell me they've got a serious problem with closing. They don't have a closing problem. When I dig into it I always find that they've clearly got problems earlier in their sales process. Victor Antonio says one of the ways to avoid this problem is to discuss key qualifiers, like pricing, early in the negotiation process, rather than later.

'Sometimes I insert price early because I want to qualify people. I usually say, "Let's get pricing out of the way, so we can have a good conversation about what you need."' he says.

Using the example of an international speaking gig, Victor says the conversation might go like this:

> **Seller** (Victor): It'll cost $20,000, plus my expenses.

> **Buyer**: Oh, that's way out of our ballpark. That's a lot of money.

> **Seller**: Well, let's walk through that. Let's see if it really is a lot of money.

Buyer: What do you mean?

Seller: Well, how many people are going to attend the event?

Buyer: We're going to have 200 people there.

Seller: If they can learn something that will increase their sales by one per cent, and your average product or service cost is X, the average close rate is X. If we move that up by one per cent, what would that number mean to your company? So, when you say $20,000 is expensive, it depends. Expensive in comparison to what?

Buyer: Okay. Let us think about it.

Seller: That's fine. Can I just ask whether I'm a good fit for this gig?

Buyer: Yes, you're a great fit. Everything we want to talk about, you have.

'This approach doesn't always work, but it does get the buyer thinking, "Is $20,000 really too expensive?" Usually, I'm able to close the deal. I think my close rate is sixty to seventy per cent. Would I like it higher? Of course. But sometimes, the buyer has to go back and get the necessary approvals before making a decision,' says Victor.

'There's nothing you can do, because you don't have the decision makers on the phone. But what happens, typically, is they'll go out and look at other options in the market. They see other people for, say, half the price – $10,000. They'll look at the difference in quality and say, "Okay. For $10,000 more, we can get what we really want. Or we can roll the dice with this other person."

'They'll usually come back and say, "You know what? Let's go ahead and sign the deal." I lose very few deals. I think one of the reasons for this is that I'm no longer afraid to talk about price, whereas I used to be.'

Victor makes a very valid point. Pricing used to be something we'd hide. We wouldn't have it on our websites – customers would have to call us to get a price on something. That's now changing, putting salespeople in a much better position to negotiate and close deals.

SUMMARY

That brings us to the end of Step 4. Before we move on to Step 5, here's a list of the key points to remember:

- Salespeople in this function are our most experienced and highly paid; we need them to be highly skilled black-belts in key MOFU activities.

- Effective qualifying upfront and ongoing through the sales process means we won't be wasting time on low-probability deals, and won't get surprises towards the end of the deal.

- An approach that incorporates insight selling is critical today. We have to bring insight and value from the start of the engagement and focus on moving the customer from their status quo to a much better scenario that includes our solution.

- Our biggest enemy isn't other competitors. It's 'no decision', or no change from the status quo. We need to build strong business cases for change, not just focus on our solution.

- In our conversations with potential buyers, we need to provide value for them, rather than adopt a friending strategy. We can do this by delivering insights to the customer.

- If we do a good job early and throughout the sales process the negotiations and closing at the end should be straightforward.

- Professional buyers are trained to simplify deals as much as possible so that they can focus on price. A seller's job is to complexify the deal as much as possible so the buyer can no longer compare products based solely on price.

Step 5: Leverage the Customer Experience and Referral Selling

'A satisfied customer is the best business strategy of all.'

MICHAEL LEBOEUF

Under the traditional sales model, customers had less leverage with salespeople. So, when we were selling to them, we would really bring them into our own process and drive them through that. Now, with the buyer being so much more empowered and having so much knowledge, it's really important that we work around how *they* want to operate. That's a huge shift that companies have had to respond to.

And it leads us to the concept of customer experience, or CX. I recently did a Google search on this term. Google has a feature that allows you to check the popularity of different terms over an extended time period. In the last ten years, the term 'customer experience', or 'CX', has skyrocketed in terms of popularity.

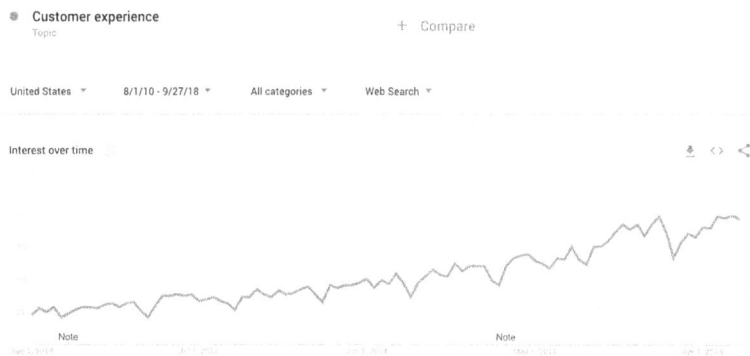

Figure 29: Customer experience, Source: Google Trends

So, why is customer experience so important? The primary reason is that it boosts retention rates. If customers receive great customer experience, they're more likely to buy from us again. According to NewVoice, fifty per cent of customers use a company more frequently after a positive customer experience, while Zendesk states that twenty-four per cent of customers continue to seek out vendors for two-plus years following a good experience. As a result, delivering an outstanding customer experience is crucial, particularly as it becomes increasingly difficult to win new accounts.

Customers are putting up more barriers to entry, doing their research online, and avoiding salespeople more effectively as each year goes by. At the same time, many companies are focused on CX, including our competitors, which means their accounts are more protected against potential poaches, making the barriers to new account acquisition even higher. Yet I still see many sales leaders banking heavily on new account business to achieve growth goals. For many, winning new business has become the shiny object of the sales world.

While there's no doubt we need to focus on customer acquisition, it should be part of an overall strategy that puts customer retention and growth directly at the centre. The path to profitability and sustainable growth is through maximising our existing accounts first and foremost. Here are nine reasons why:

- **Cost efficiency**. Salesforce estimates it is six to seven times more expensive to gain a new customer than it is to keep an existing one.

- **Higher profitability**. There's a lot of leverage to the bottom line by growing existing customers. According to research undertaken by Bain & Company, increasing customer retention by five per cent can impact profitability by between twenty-five per cent and ninety-five per cent.

- **Better close rates**. Research shows a sixty to eighty per cent close rate for existing customers, compared to just ten to thirty per cent for new accounts. This will obviously flow through to sales productivity and profitability.

- **Account acquisition is getting tougher**. New account acquisition has been getting progressively harder in the past few years, as buyers become more adept at avoiding salespeople. Even when buyers are ready to engage, it's often too late to really influence their direction.

- **A stronger, more sustainable business**. Existing customers should always be a large part of your business. According to Gartner, eighty per cent of your revenue will come from just twenty per cent of your existing customers.

- **A powerful differentiator**. Many organisations (read: your competitors) do not get this right and take existing customers for granted. There are few companies that do this really well.

- **Build your war chest**. Having a growing and satisfied account base helps you build the profitability to be aggressive on the account acquisition side. You will need deep pockets to sustain acquisition efforts and unseat entrenched competitors. New accounts are getting more difficult and expensive to win, so this needs to be funded by serving existing customers extremely well.

- **It's mandatory for survival**. If nurturing and growing your relationships with existing customers is the path to growth and profitability, then the inverse is also true. Lose good, valuable and profitable customers on a regular basis, and your business will be negatively impacted. Thinking that you can replace lost customers with new ones all the time is like pouring water into a leaky bucket.

- **A powerful referral and reference engine**. Satisfied existing customers are the best source of referrals and reference sites. In fact, this is the most powerful lead-generation engine for winning new accounts. Again, this is even more critical as the barriers to winning new business get higher.

When we're inside an account already, we're in a very unique position to keep competitors out. To sell more. Understand more about the customer's business. Bring them more insight. Bring them more value by selling them other products. That's a huge advantage that we must leverage to the maximum.

And with the shift to subscription models, where customers are often making monthly payments for a product or service, it is very easy for customers to turn off your product or service and switch to something else. The software industry has totally gone in this direction with SaaS being the predominant way to access software now. If you use Office 365, you're probably paying by month, like I am. If you use any Adobe products, that used to be $1,000 for a licence. Now, it's forty dollars a month. Even companies that sell hardware are increasingly selling a bundle of hardware and services for a monthly fee. The mindset now is, 'We've got to give great service to get the renewal.'

Our sales process has to be about not just getting the sale, but about delivering exceptional customer service, so that we boost renewals and create customer advocates. We want the customer so excited about our product or service, and the support they're receiving, that they will go into the market and advocate actively on behalf of our solution.

Developing the customer success function

We spoke about the customer success function in Step 1, and how it fits into the new sales structure. However, as part of our discussion on creating and leveraging a great customer experience, it's worth revisiting here.

The customer success function – which sits alongside the prospecting and lead-gen and core sales functions – is designed to help customers extract maximum value from our products and services. The team is focused on delighting existing customers, which in turn should drive renewals and expansion.

However, unlike the other key sales functions, the customer success function is reasonably new in the sales profession. So, how does it differ from the traditional notion of customer service? For a start, customer success is a proactive function with the goal of helping the customer successfully implement and extract maximum value from what they have bought from us. This compares to the reactive customer service function who respond to customer issues as they come up. While this is still a critical function, it is just one part of the customer experience.

There are a couple of common models of customer success in both the B2C and B2B landscape. The first is a premium support model where the customer pays for a higher level of proactive support, while the second is just included as part of the ongoing account management model. With cloud products, for example, customers typically get a basic level of support included with a monthly subscription, which involves fixing problems when they arise. If the product or service isn't performing, the user logs a ticket and eventually the problem gets handled. This is the customer service component.

Those who want additional services or support will often pay a premium. This is often known as customer success. A customer success manager, or CSM, is deeply immersed in that particular product or service. As a customer, they're in front of you all the time. Meeting with you. Talking about the new features and functions. Understanding your business and working out how the product can help you meet your business objectives. They become the interface between what you're trying to achieve as a business and how the technology can help you achieve that.

The number one metric of just about every customer success team is customer satisfaction. That's typically measured either through a net promoter score, or more directly through a customer satisfaction survey. The second key metric is renewals. From a business perspective, the reason you have a customer success team is to ensure you have high renewal rates with your customers.

When setting up a customer success function, here are six key tips:

- Really understand what you're trying to achieve with your customer success program. Most companies are structuring the customer success function to focus primarily on the premium support model discussed earlier. That really dictates how you set up your team. So, understand what you're trying to achieve.

- Identify your key drivers. What are the KPIs for your CSMs? What are the metrics that you're going to derive to inform those KPIs? That can drive you down a very data-driven path to customer success, or you can take a much more people-oriented approach, which is much more focused on feel, intent, net promoter scores and customer satisfaction surveys. Once again, that really dictates how you set up your program.

- Determine how you're going to segment your customers. The default approach today is that customers are segmented by size or, in some cases, complexity. So, the large customers who bring in the majority of your revenue clearly get more of the CSM's time and attention. You need to define how you're going to set up that approach. How are you going to move customers from a scale environment to a high-touch environment?

- Allocate CSMs as early as possible. That way, even before the contract is signed, the customer can start meeting with their CSM and the salesperson can say, 'When you sign, this person will be your CSM. This is what they'll be doing.' Start to introduce the concept and the function of the CSM before the contract is signed.

   Remember, there's lots of activity required in the start-up phase, or implementation, of a new contract. The CSM can help smooth out some of the kinks that always happen when you take on a new contract. So, the earlier we can get a CSM assigned and engaged, the better.

- Set clear expectations for everyone involved, particularly the customer. It has to be clear that if you know a customer is not going to get a lot of time with a CSM – because they're just not big enough or they're not complex enough to warrant it – that the core sales team isn't overselling the amount of time they'll get.

   For example, you can't tell a customer they're guaranteed to get a fulltime, onsite CSM and then, as soon as the contract is signed, have someone call the customer only once a month. You've got to make sure that everyone's expectations are the same.

- Form a united front. The relationship between the core sales team and the customer success function is critical. One of the approaches we see far too often is where the core sales team signs a deal. Then, as soon as the ink is dry, they just throw the contract over to the CSM and say, 'It's yours now.' Then they move on to the next opportunity.

I spoke to Chris Connelly, who is the vice president of customer success management for SAP across Asia Pacific & Japan and was previously in a similar role for Salesforce, who were one of the pioneering companies in this space. He gave me some great input for this section of the book, and one powerful point he made was, 'The best accounts that I've seen managed have had the Account Executives driving regular internal catch-ups with all of the internal parties to provide a unified approach to that customer. I really can't emphasise enough how critical that combined account team approach is.'

As Chris emphasises, it's essential that the core sales team and the customer success function are united. They should be partnering to achieve the same goals and be presenting a consistent front to the customer. So, while the sales team is clearly focused on new opportunities, upsells and cross-sells, it's critical that the CSM is part of those meetings, providing on-the-ground advice, or an update on what's happening on a day-to-day basis with that customer.

Creating a great customer experience

Bernd Schmitt, who is considered a world authority on customer experience, describes customer experience management as 'the process of strategically managing a customer's entire experience with a product or company.'

There are two key points to remember here. First, customer experience management is a strategic process and should therefore be embedded in everything we do. Second, it's a process that travels the entire length and breadth of the customer's journey, from start to finish.

There are four key steps to creating a great customer experience:

- Gather insights
- Find new opportunities for the customer
- Grow the customer's product utilisation
- Scale the customer experience

Here's a breakdown of all four steps.

1.   Gather insights

As discussed in Step 4, insight gathering already happens in the middle of the funnel. However, it's important to continue gathering insights after we've made the sale. In doing so, we can find opportunities to give the customer more value, through upsells, special offers and so on. If we don't, this is more likely to lead to dissatisfied customers who aren't getting what they want from the product.

So, how do we develop insights at this stage? I recommend having customer success teams dedicated to your biggest clients, so you can easily gather utilisation data. For example, when I worked at Targus, we had ongoing relationships with the largest PC vendors where we supplied either exclusively or a large majority of their laptop cases. We often had dedicated account management teams embedded with these customers, in what was really a combined customer success and sales function.

Being embedded like this we yielded great insight into the trends in the customers' businesses, including the key growth opportunities in our category.

To gather insights, we really wanted to understand how many laptops they were shipping in different geographies and channels, and then how many laptop cases each office is shipping. Then we'd get an attach rate. We often found a big disparity, with some groups selling one for one but others only selling at a twenty or thirty per cent attach rate, or as low as ten to fifteen per cent.

2. Find new opportunities for the customer

These insights then lead to new opportunities for the customer, such as better ways to use the product, reaching out to other parts of the business that could be using the product, and upsell opportunities.

As a result, this grows customer business, increases product utilisation and drives renewals. Building on the Targus example, if some sales groups were only selling laptop cases at a rate of ten to fifteen per cent, there was a clear opportunity to increase utilisation.

3. Grow the customer's product utilisation

Once we've identified new opportunities for the customer, we can use these to grow the customer's product utilisation. By providing more value to the customer in this way, we increase customer satisfaction and boost profits.

How do we position these newly found opportunities in a way that delivers more value to the customer? It could be as simple as saying, 'This group is using all these features of the product and getting these benefits. This other group is *not* using those features and therefore not getting those same benefits.'

Going back to the Targus example, we might present to the management of these key accounts that there could be a fifty per cent upside in a certain business unit if they adopted the attach rate practices of some of the other groups. We would also put a dollar figure around it – for instance, it could be worth $2 million in revenue to them with a significant margin. And, again leveraging our insight and experience, we would develop a specific attach rate program that they could run and we would even contribute to the marketing funding since it created upside for all of us. So we were using our incumbent status to proactively come up with insightful solutions that generated upside for the client.

4. Scale the customer experience

After completing this process successfully with one customer, we can start implementing it with other customers, thus increasing revenue exponentially. For example, let's say Salesforce was selling into Telstra. No doubt Salesforce is present in a lot of other telcos around the world and has therefore built up expertise on how to drive utilisation in this industry.

Salesforce will therefore be asking itself questions like, 'What's the best practice for utilisation? Which features are being used by telcos? Is there a telco that's using ninety per cent of our features, across all their sales functions?' Then, Salesforce would highlight value to Telstra by saying something like, 'Do you know you can change how you provide customer quotes? You can change how you manage your pipeline to make it more effective.'

Salesforce would then highlight a tangible benefit – whether it's closing more sales quicker, or removing steps from Telstra's sales process, or saving every Telstra salesperson an hour each week. Because Salesforce has already been through this process with other telcos, it is easily replicated with Telstra.

A strategic approach to referral selling

The goal of delivering a great customer experience is to create happy customers who will continue to work with us and will buy from us repeatedly over time. A secondary benefit, however, is that happy customers become the greatest advocates of a brand, or a specific product or service. They tell stories and they make recommendations. They have the power to influence other potential customers with their enthusiasm for adoption, and therefore should be seen as a core element of long-term strategic growth.

In a Nielsen study, ninety-two per cent of respondents trusted referrals from people they knew. The same study revealed people were four times more likely to buy when referred by someone they knew. With more and more noise in today's marketplace, and more information competing for buyers' time and attention, this isn't surprising.

However, the benefits of referrals go far beyond increased customer acquisition. According to the Wharton School of Business, the lifetime value for referred customers is sixteen per cent higher than non-referred customers. Referred customers are also eighteen per cent less likely to leave than non-referred customers, showing referrals can have a big impact on customer retention rates.

With this in mind, we can't just leave referrals to chance. We can't just provide a great customer experience and hope the customer sends more people our way. We need a structured process to generate referral sales.

It's worth noting that under the old sales model, structured referral selling wasn't possible because sales teams were always focused on that quarter's numbers. In the new model, customer success is a separate function, with the customer success manager accountable for referrals.

With that in mind, are you actively seeking referrals from your existing customers? Do you have a structured referral program in place? Do you track referrals through your pipeline? Do you discuss referral activities in your sales meetings? If not, don't worry. For the remainder of this section, I'll show you how to boost referrals and drive a healthy pipeline of referred customers.

Create customer advocates

It's not enough just to achieve a sale with a customer. On the contrary, we have not done our job until our customers are satisfied to the point of becoming willing advocates for us. We must start our engagement with the customer with this goal in mind, and gear our sales incentives and structures towards creating customer advocates.

So, how do we do this exactly? The key is to look at it from the customer's perspective. What's in it for them? Hootsuite's Ambassador Program is a great example of a customer advocacy program. Stretching across the globe in over fifty countries, Hootsuite's 500-plus ambassadors are described as 'the heart of Hootsuite's community'. There are clear incentives for becoming a Hootsuite ambassador:

- Gain recognition by being able to share your ambassador position on LinkedIn and other online profiles

- Have the chance to impact new product developments through beta testing and sharing feedback with Hootsuite

- Get the chance to access Hootsuite social media education products and receive the most up-to-date social media training

So, what incentives can we offer to create our own customer advocates, or ambassadors? We've got to think about what's important to a lot of the senior people in our customer base. What can we offer them that really makes them feel close to us? We might put them on our customer advisory council, for example. We might give them secret advance briefings on new products coming out. We might give them access to top executives in our company. The possibilities are endless.

Leverage a high point

There's a misconception that we should wait until a product or service has been installed, or is in use, before we start asking for referrals. But it isn't always necessary to wait so long.

In fact, customers often feel very positive towards us and our solution at the end of a long evaluation or when they are signing the contract.

This is an obvious 'high point' for the customer and is therefore a good time to ask for a referral. Other high points might be at installation, or once the benefits of the solution are realised. It really depends on the customer, the product or service, and the industry.

According to business guru Ray Silverstein, we shouldn't feel sheepish about asking for referrals, because customers won't give us referrals unless we deserve them (this is why it's so important to deliver an outstanding customer experience). In fact, we should make it a habit to ask for referrals.

Be direct and specific

When asking for referrals, it's important to be as direct and specific as possible. If we are too general or broad in our request, then we make it difficult for the customer to understand what we are looking for. We need to guide the customer to what we want, and frame our request in the most helpful and constructive way.

For example, a less effective way to ask for a referral is to say, 'Bob, can you refer me to anyone who could use our product?' This is very broad and doesn't guide the customer at all. As a result, Bob will be thinking, 'What do you mean by "anyone"?'

A more effective approach is, 'Bob, do you know anyone in your industry, in a similar role to yourself, that you could introduce me to?' This way, we narrow down the field by industry and role. These two additional filters make it easier for Bob to answer the question, because he knows exactly what we're looking for.

An even better approach is, 'Bob, I know you're well connected in the finance industry. I wonder if you might be able to introduce me to one or two other network managers who have been facing similar challenges with managing security on mobile devices.' In this final example, we've identified four criteria of what we are looking for. As a result, it is much easier for Bob to pinpoint the right target.

Develop a referral program

While almost everyone acknowledges the huge benefits of referral selling, very few set up formal programs or processes to prioritise it. To really drive growth, we need to make this a front-and-centre priority. This means creating incentives for referrals, discussing referrals in sales meetings, tracking leads from referral sources, and measuring outcomes from referral leads.

There are plenty of referral programs we can draw inspiration from. Dropbox, for example, has launched a referral program that rewards customers with product-based perks instead of monetary ones. Dropbox offers an extra 500 megabytes of free storage space to the customer who makes the referral, and to the newly referred user.

As a result of this program, Dropbox saw its membership skyrocket by about sixty per cent in a single year. Product-based discounts, perks or upgrades can make our customers more invested in our companies and more engaged with our products. This will strengthen their loyalty and likely result in more referrals.

Referral selling has so many benefits that there's no reason not to turbocharge our efforts in this area. Build on your customer advocacy and referral selling programs as you go, by working out what works best for you and your team, as well as your customers.

SUMMARY

That brings us to the end of Step 5. Before we move on to Step 6, here's a list of the key points to remember:

The business case for creating customer advocates and generating referrals is really strong: lower cost of sales, better close rates, higher spend and more.

- CX is trending very strongly. This means our competitors are doing their best to keep their customers, increasing the barriers for account acquisition.

- While there's no doubt we need to focus on customer acquisition, the path to profitability and sustainable growth is through maximising our existing accounts first and foremost.

- The Customer Success function is critical to our success in building advocates and generating referrals. It is a proactive function focused on ensuring customers receive great value from usage of our product.

- There are four key steps to creating a great customer experience:
  - Gather insights
  - Find new opportunities for the customer
  - Grow the customer's product utilisation
  - Scale the customer experience

- Develop a formal advocacy and customer referral program. Don't leave it to chance.

- In order to boost referrals and drive a healthy pipeline of referred customers, we need to create customer advocates, request the referral at a high point in their experience, be direct and specific with the request, and develop a formalised referral program.

Step 6: Invest in Collaboration and Stakeholder Management

'Great things in business are never done by one person, they're done by a team of people.'

STEVE JOBS

The new sales structure is built on three core functions: prospecting and lead generation, core sales, and customer success. For the new sales structure to succeed, collaboration is a crucial element. This includes collaboration within the sales team, across the different functions (prospecting and lead generation, middle of the funnel, and customer success), and across the business as a whole.

There are multiple studies showing good salespeople have strong internal networks. For example, VoloMetrix studied the sales force of a large B2B software company using six quarters of quota attainment data for several thousand employees. It then correlated this against eighteen months of key performance indicators, like time spent with a customer or manager, the size and cross-functionality of an internal network, how important a given employee is within an internal network, and time spent in the presence of senior leadership.

They found that top performers had thirty to forty per cent larger internal networks than average. In particular they had wide and deep relationships with support staff, had strong links with management and invested time proactively cultivating their internal networks.

One of the reasons top performers exceed their quotas is because of their ability to get things done internally. This is even more important in the new sales structure, as sales no longer owns the entire customer relationship. With marketing and customer service involved, we need to leverage and collaborate with those groups to be effective.

Top sales performers have **30–40%** larger internal networks than average

The key to strong collaboration is effective stakeholder management. To understand why this is important, allow me to use an analogy.

We're all familiar with the classic movie scene where someone is waiting for a table at a restaurant, and someone else arrives after them and gets one straightaway. How does this happen? The usurper knows the restaurant manager, or one of the wait staff, and has invested in that relationship over time. Then, all it takes is a nod or a wink, and possibly a discreet tip, for them to get what they wanted instantly. Meanwhile, the person who arrived first is still waiting for a table, feeling frustrated, and perhaps even wondering what they did wrong.

This happens in companies too. There are finite resources available, which means effective stakeholder management is absolutely critical if we want our sales teams to succeed.

When we invest in collaboration and stakeholder management, we're more likely to receive the support and resources we need. In particular, when we develop trust with our stakeholders, we're less likely to get second-guessed or blocked. This leads to more open, efficient communication, making it easier for us to do our jobs – and do them well. In turn, greater collaboration and stakeholder management leads to better sales results, since our effectiveness is multiplied when we effectively lead others.

In contrast, if we don't invest in collaboration and stakeholder management, we'll have to fight for support and resources. We'll also be crippled by inefficient communication, making it much harder for us to do our jobs well. And perhaps worst of all, we run the risk of confusing or irritating customers, and wasting valuable resources.

For example, I recently worked with a client who had set up a new prospecting team separate from the core sales team. Unfortunately, there was poor alignment between the two functions. The prospecting team kept calling existing customers and asking them basic questions, or pressing them for information even though they were already established customers. This is a classic case of left hand and right hand not knowing what the other is doing. It proved extremely costly, since all that prospecting effort was a waste of time and money, and did significant damage to those customer relationships.

So, how can we ensure strong collaboration and stakeholder management? In this step, I'll outline a stakeholder management framework we can follow, and, as an extension of that, how to build trust with our stakeholders.

A proven framework for stakeholder management

Effective stakeholder management has always served sales teams well. A core part of our role is ensuring we have in place the necessary internal resources for us to do our jobs successfully. As I touched on in the introduction, I believe this is even more important as our role, and other roles, becomes more specialised. We now have to work closely with other functions who are also touching the customer, as well as external stakeholders.

But how many salespeople and sales leaders proactively manage their stakeholders, or have a strategy in place to build that strong support network? What we will discuss here is a proven four-step framework for developing strong stakeholder relationships.

1. Create a stakeholder map

The first step is to identify and map out internal and external stakeholders. Internal stakeholders are entities within the business, including employees, managers, the chairperson and board of directors, and investors. External stakeholders are entities outside the business, who have an interest in, or are affected by, the business's performance. This includes customers, regulators, investors and suppliers.

Figure 30 is a stakeholder map for one of my coaching clients who is the Asia Pacific president for a US-based technology vendor. The organisation is quite complex, with many stakeholders and also many responsibilities pulling at them and demanding their time. Without an effective stakeholder management and prioritisation system, they could not be effective in their role and would burn out in no time.

EXTERNAL STAKEHOLDERS

Customers
- Corporate
- Government
- Distribution
- Retail
- Online

All in many countries

Government
Relations
Regulators
Legal

Advertising
& PR Agencies
Consultants

Business
Partners &
Alliances

Chairman
& Board

CEO

President
Americas

President
EMEA

Global
CFO

Global Head
Operations

Global Head
HR

Global Head
Marketing

Global Head
Products

**President
Asia Pacific**

Assistant

INTERNAL STAKEHOLDERS

CFO
Asia Pacific

VP
Operations

VP
HR

VP
Marketing

VP
ASEAN / Korea

VP
ANZ

VP
Japan

VP
India

VP
China

KEY RESPONSIBILIES

Sales/ Marketing	Financials	People	Operations	Future	Corporate Responsibiliy	Personal
Revenue	Expenses	Communications	Delivery	Strategy	Environment	Work / life balance
Margin	Profit	Motivation	Inventory	Planning	Diversity	Health
Product performance	Controls	Staff development	Customer service	Product development	Community	Family
Productivity	Compliance	Engagement	Quality	Consumer research	Industry development	Staff development
Sales planning	Audit	Bench strength	Efficiency	Org. development		
Brand		Hiring		Facilities		

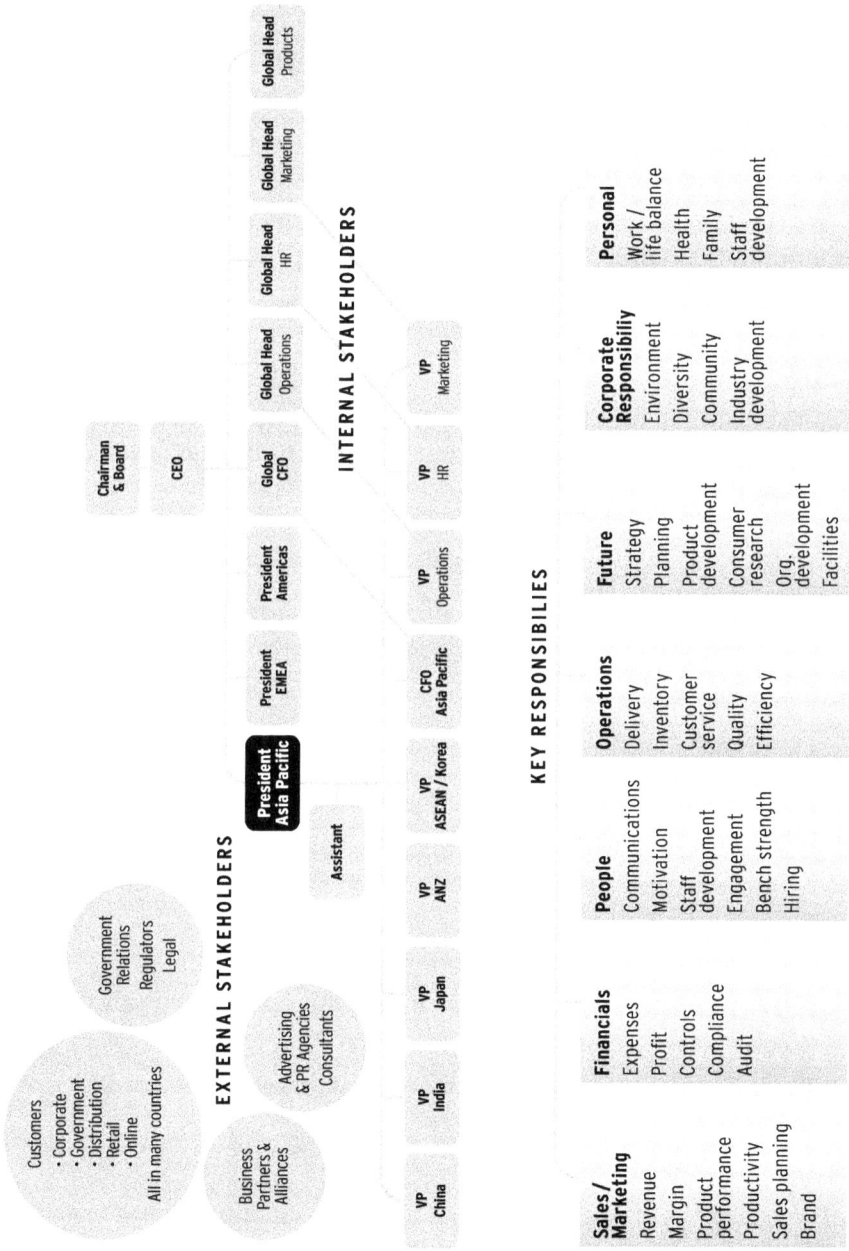

Figure 30: Stakeholder map

The life of sales leaders is extremely intense with many demands on your time. For the sales team, the marketing group is essential, as is the customer success team. Managers across different divisions are also key to the sales team's success. Outside the business, the most obvious stakeholders are the customers, but beyond that, it's also important to consider business partners, alliances and channel partners. Basically, any individual or entity that will help you win business, or affect your business in some way. On my map, for example, I've included government as an external stakeholder.

Here are four questions to help you identify key stakeholders (both internal and external):

- Does the stakeholder have a fundamental impact on your organisation's performance? (Required response: yes.)

- Can you clearly identify what you want from the stakeholder? (Required response: yes.)

- Is the relationship dynamic? In order words, do you want it to grow? (Required response: yes.)

- Can you exist without or easily replace the stakeholder? (Required response: no.)

Once you've identified your key stakeholders, draw an organisation map, starting with yourself. Where do you fit? Then, map out all the people next to you, and above and below you. Then, you have to prioritise the external stakeholders. Who are the key people you deal with, externally? Map them accordingly.

2. Analyse key stakeholders

The key to analysing your stakeholders is to figure out what's important to them. In other words, what are their goals? When we understand our stakeholders' goals, we can:

- Identify and focus on common goals

- Understand where our goals diverge and where we might need to trade support to achieve our own objectives

Here's an example of how it might work for a sales director and a field marketing manager. As we can see in this example their goals are quite different. Ideally we would want to see some strong overlap in goals but the reality in many companies is more like this.

Position	Key goals
Sales director	Meet unit sales goal
	Win three large deals
	Improve overall margins
	Build next quarter's pipeline
	Boost sales productivity
	Oversee channel development
	Further career goals
Field marketing manager	Improve marketing ROI
	Improve cost savings
	Boost event attendance
	Oversee digital transition
	Further career goals

Figure 31: Stakeholder analysis

Let's say the sales director needs marketing support to drive some programs to achieve his or her unit goal for the quarter, but this is not one of the marketing team's specific goals. However, the sales director can help marketing get strong attendance at their events, which *is* one of the marketing team's key goals.

So, here is a great opportunity for a trade. Maybe in return for a $50,000 marketing program that will drive more units, the sales director will instruct every member of his team to get ten customers to attend an important upcoming event. In reality, it might not be as clear-cut as this. The idea is to build trust over time (more on this in the next section), so that when you need something, you can get it.

3. Prioritise stakeholders

By prioritising stakeholders, you'll be more effective in determining where to spend your time and energy. In other words, which stakeholders are going to give you the biggest bang for your buck? Which stakeholders are most likely, or most able, to move things in your favour?

This matrix is designed to help you categorise your stakeholders, and prioritise accordingly. You can see there are four quadrants – 'Keep Satisfied', 'Actively Engage', 'Monitor' and 'Keep Informed'. The vertical axis represents influence, while the horizontal axis represents interest or availability.

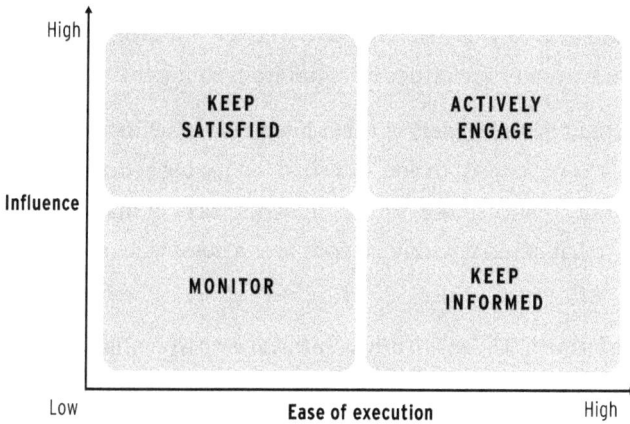

Figure 32: Stakeholder prioritisation

So, which stakeholders belong in each quadrant? Here's a brief overview:

- **Actively Engage**: Key decision makers with direct involvement in your team.

- For a sales leader, this could include:

  - Your direct boss

  - Your marketing peer

  - Your marketing peer's boss

  - The finance head responsible for the expenses and profitability of your team, who is likely approving deals and key expenses in the business

  - The HR and recruitment head who will help keep your team fully staffed with high-quality salespeople and will also help execute people development programs for your team

- **Keep Satisfied**: Key decision makers who are not directly involved with your team or are difficult to maintain contact with.

  These could be the leaders of other business segments or functions that may be of interest to you, but there's not a big benefit in investing a lot of time there (so, for example, the head of manufacturing or exports). It could possibly be your boss's boss, who is focused on other priorities.

- **Keep Informed**: Those with less influence on you and your team, but who have a high interest and may want more of your time than you can give.

  This would include the marketing team or overlay sales functions that want your mindshare and support in order to meet their own goals. We could easily fill our whole schedule if we agreed to engage with every one of these people. Having said that, they are important to our overall success, and we want to keep them motivated and aligned with what we're doing.

- **Monitor**: Anyone not directly involved with you and your team, with a low interest.

  This includes other team leaders who could indirectly impact the success or otherwise of your team.

4. Develop tailored communication strategies

To ensure you invest the right amount of effort into each stakeholder relationship, it's important to develop communication strategies for each of the groups identified in the previous section. This will ensure every stakeholder relationship is as productive as possible.

With this in mind, here are the actions to take with each stakeholder group:

- **Actively Engage: Set up consistent touchpoints**. We want to be having solid one-on-one engagement, and ongoing multi-thread and multi-channel dialogue, with all of these stakeholders on an ongoing basis.

- **Keep Satisfied: Requires a light touch to maintain satisfaction**. We want to be respectful and responsive to any of these senior people, and also keep them updated via email on what we're doing as it applies to them. For example, we might share a case study or a sales best practice that could be used elsewhere.

- **Keep Informed: Actively keep informed with emails, reports, presentations and so on**. We need to find efficient ways to keep these stakeholders engaged and informed. Beyond the obvious channels like email, reports and presentations, perhaps we could include them in some of our weekly and monthly forums, and delegate some of our team members to be the nominated interface between our team and theirs.

- **Monitor: Keep monitoring in case their level of influence or interest changes**. Organisations and executives are always changing and getting shifted around, so we always need to be aware of when someone is coming into our orbit who could be important for our success. It never hurts to be proactive when someone is moving into a role that is relevant to our team.

Building trust with stakeholders

Trust is a crucial component of any company's success – not only in the context of effective stakeholder management but across the board. When people trust each other, they're more productive. According to an article by the *Harvard Business Review*, which compares the employees of high-trust companies to those of low-trust companies, the former are seventy-four per cent less stressed, fifty per cent more productive, 106 per cent more energised and seventy-six per cent more engaged. They also enjoy their jobs sixty per cent more, are seventy per cent more aligned with their companies' purpose, and feel sixty-six per cent closer to their colleagues.

Just imagine if, as a sales leader, I went to a member of the marketing team and asked for his support on running an event around an initiative I was working on. If this initiative succeeded, it would potentially be $10 million to $20 million in revenue, so it would be extremely significant for my career. For the marketing person to run this event, though, he must have a high degree of confidence and trust in me. He needs to trust that I will deliver what I say I will. If I don't, he will have wasted valuable marketing resources and diverted from his boss's priorities for nothing. There's a high level of risk for this stakeholder, which is why trust is everything.

Salespeople who don't cultivate strong working relationships, and a high level of trust, can really fall down here. They ask for support, and they get it the first time. But then they don't come through with the deal, or they don't come through with the numbers. As a result, the second or third time they ask for support, they don't get it.

Nothing works without trust. Let me give you another example to highlight the impact trust has on our ability to do our job efficiently and successfully. I have a good feeling about a customer, but I need to use additional resources to get them on board. If I've built up trust in my working relationships, maybe it will only take a one-minute conversation to get the resources I need. If I don't have trust, or that trust has been eroded somehow, then maybe it will never happen. Or I'll be asked to present a business case, explaining why I need the equipment. Instead of a one-minute conversation, the process could take a week, or two weeks, or even longer. That's the difference between having trust and not having it.

So, how do we build trust?

First off, we need to dedicate some time and effort to cultivating those relationships. This means understanding the goals of the other parties, and thinking about how we can help them reach their goals as well as our own.

Then, we need to be delivering consistently. We can't win the deal every time, but we need to have a pretty decent hit rate. This is achieved by following through on our commitments, always doing our best, and looking out for the other party. In other words, not leaving them high and dry.

B2B sales productivity expert John Cousineau has developed a trust-building framework for B2B sales, inspired by a more general trust-building framework developed by Professor Paul Zak, founding director of the US-based Center for Neuroeconomics Studies. Here are five additional ways to build trust:

1. **Measure and recognise progress.** The more frequently people experience a sense of progress with their work, the more productive they're likely to be in the long run. So, to this end, we need to measure and recognise progress.

   Neuroscience studies show recognition has the largest effect on trust when it occurs immediately after a goal has been set, when it comes from peers, and when it's tangible, unexpected, personal and public. In addition to giving top performers a platform for their success, it inspires others to aim high as well. We can do this by having daily progress updates, celebrating individual victories, and learning from these victories as a team.

2. **Give staff autonomy.** Nearly half of employees would give up a twenty per cent raise for greater control over how they work, according to a Citigroup and LinkedIn survey. So, once employees have been trained, we should trust them to figure things out on their own. In addition to building trust, autonomy also promotes innovation, as people are free to try different approaches. Post-deal debriefs allow teams to share how positive deviations came about, so that others can build on their success.

3. **Share information openly.** According to a Gallup study of two and a half million manager-led teams in 195 countries, workforce engagement improved when supervisors had some form of daily communication with direct reports. Yet only forty per cent of employees report they are well informed about their company's goals, strategies and tactics. By openly sharing company plans with our teams, we reduce uncertainty and stress about where the company is headed and why, and build trust as a result.

4. **Encourage social connections.** A study of software engineers in Silicon Valley found those who connected with others, and helped them with their projects, not only earned the respect and trust of their peers but were also more productive themselves.

   We can help people build social connections by organising company lunches, after-work events and team-building activities. Adding some sort of team challenge to the mix will speed up the bonding process and help to build trust.

5. **Show vulnerability.** According to Professor Zak, leaders in high-trust workplaces ask for help from colleagues, instead of simply instructing them to complete tasks. This stimulates oxytocin production, increasing trust and cooperation. Far from coming across as inept, asking for help signifies a secure leader. So, if we don't have the answer, we should involve our teams to seek it out together.

SUMMARY

That brings us to the end of Step 6. Before we move on to the final step, here's a list of the key points to remember:

- Top-performing salespeople have thirty to forty per cent larger internal networks, and proactively spend time developing them.

- One of the reasons top performers exceed their quotas is because of their ability to get things done internally. This is even more important in the new sales structure, as sales needs to partner with many other functions.

- Trust is a crucial component of any company's success – not only in the context of effective stakeholder management but across the board. When people trust each other, they're more productive.

- Employees of high-trust companies are seventy-four per cent less stressed, fifty per cent more productive, 106 per cent more energised and seventy-six per cent more engaged.

- So, how do we build trust? Firstly, we need to dedicate some time and effort to cultivating those relationships. Then, we need to be delivering consistently.

Step 7: Focus on Continuous Change and Improvement

*'The world hates change, yet it is the only thing
that has brought progress.'*

CHARLES KETTERING

This whole book is about change – the changes happening within the market and with buying processes, and the internal structures, processes and initiatives we need to implement to stay relevant and keep winning. If we want our teams to survive and thrive in today's sales landscape, we must be proactive about internal change, which means constantly looking for ways to improve how things are done in order to get better results. We must facilitate continuous change and improvement not only in our teams, but more broadly across our companies.

It is critical for the leader to be leading these changes and to be actively involved from their development through to their execution. This shows your team your seriousness and commitment. After all, if team members don't see their leaders taking new initiatives seriously, then why should they? It is also the only way to ensure success. Change has many enemies and there will always be barriers to overcome, so it is important that the leader is there to guide, support and keep everyone motivated.

This is a great opportunity for sales leaders to be a proactive driving force in taking their companies forward. With the rise of the CMO, the marketing function has taken on a much more important role in B2B businesses. Meanwhile, we have seen the rise of the CXO with the accumulation of wide responsibilities to drive change across the organisation. It is now time for sales leaders to be equally active in driving positive change.

As we covered earlier, many of our sales structures are more than 100 years old, and even the more recent methodologies might be twenty to thirty years old. Today, things are moving much more quickly. The market is changing. Customers are changing. Products are changing. Technology is changing. As a result, we need to be very skilled at managing and driving change within our teams.

But how many of us really have a deep knowledge of managing and driving change successfully? Even though managing change effectively is a key competency for modern leaders, very few are actually good at it.

According to the *Harvard Business Review*, less than one third of employees understand their company's strategy. Researchers from the University of Technology in Sydney asked employees of twenty major Australian corporations, with clearly articulated public strategies, to identify their employer's strategy from six choices. Just twenty-nine per cent chose correctly, and the question was multiple choice!

In other words, more than seventy per cent of employees don't understand their company's strategy. This means they don't understand the changes taking place and why, and their role in facilitating those changes. This can hinder our companies' long-term survival and success.

This is then exacerbated by the fact that it's common for senior management to launch initiatives but fail to follow through properly. Or they launch a new initiative and expect everyone to support it, without explaining why. Then they wonder why people aren't supporting it, or, worse, people look like they're supporting it but they're not. This results in wasted resources and misalignment, which can be very costly.

For today's leaders, it's no longer enough to come up with great plans, or be a great communicator, or lead from the front and break down barriers. To be successful at driving change, we need to be competent across all three of these areas. In addition, if we want to get ahead of the competition, we need to implement more changes, more regularly. The faster we can absorb change and execute on change, the better we can perform in the marketplace.

If we fail to embrace and facilitate constant change, over time we'll become less effective, as our old processes won't work any more. As market, company and customer conditions continue to evolve, we'll get left behind.

So, as sales leaders, how do we facilitate continuous change and improvement? In this final step, we'll discuss how to decide which opportunities to pursue, how to prioritise time to pursue those initiatives, and how to manage the process of change via a change management framework.

Deciding which opportunities to pursue

There will always be countless opportunities we could go after, and changes we could make with our teams. However, in order to get the best results, we need to be selective about which opportunities we pursue, and which ones we don't.

If we try to pursue every single opportunity that presents itself, we'll end up doing a mediocre job because we've spread ourselves too thin, and may neglect our regular tasks in favour of pursuing 'the next big thing'. We're also more likely to overspend or run out of funds before we achieve our goals. And perhaps worst of all, we'll burn out our teams, who will be unable to do their work effectively and will be frustrated that they aren't getting results – or being rewarded as a consequence.

One tool I like to use to compare various opportunities is this simple opportunity matrix. I find it's always good to get input from key stakeholders on which opportunities we should evaluate. This way we get some wide perspectives and are more likely to get buy-in and support as we settle on priorities.

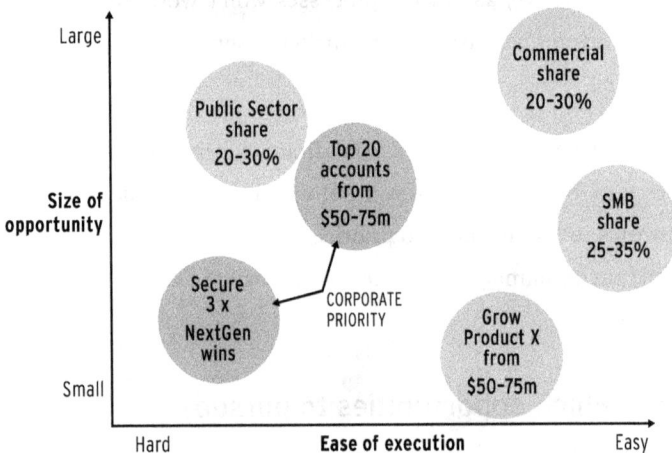

Figure 33: Opportunity matrix

The vertical axis of the opportunity matrix represents opportunity size, from small to large. The horizontal axis represents ease of execution, from hard to easy.

To complete the opportunity matrix, we line up all of those opportunities and evaluate which ones would be easiest to complete (ease of execution) and which ones would have the most impact on our business (size of opportunity). Try to rank these opportunities using the matrix, and determine how many of them you could realistically take on with your team.

The example is one that evaluates market or sales opportunities, but we could also use a similar matrix to evaluate internal opportunities. There are so many things we could be doing to improve our sales operations, but only so much change we can do effectively, so we need to highly prioritise and focus our efforts. For example, are we going to change how we hire? Are we going to change our sales structure? Are we going to develop a prospecting function? Are we going to change our CRM? Or implement a new reporting system? We should evaluate these types of changes very closely too, understanding the effort required and the potential upside benefits of doing them.

There's one more point I'd like to make before we move on. On the opportunity matrix example, a couple of the opportunities are starred, with the star representing a corporate priority. These denote opportunities that, for whatever reason, the company expects our teams to pursue, regardless of size or ease of execution. For example, the opportunity in the bottom left corner – labelled 'Secure 3 x NextGen wins' – is quite small, but the team will probably have to pursue it.

Prioritising time to pursue new initiatives

Driving change and new initiatives can easily go off track – there are so many risks and a high failure rate. Therefore, it is absolutely essential that, as leaders, we are present through the whole process – conception, development, alignment and execution. As leaders, we need to stay fully engaged until each new initiative has built its own momentum and is embedded in the business. If you, as a leader, aren't personally involved in leading change, then it won't go anywhere, instead becoming some of the seventy per cent of initiatives that fail (according to Forbes).

However, this is easier said than done because we're already very busy and the pressures are piling up, with always-on communications, so many goals and metrics to focus on in the here and now and so many stakeholders with an interest in our business. If you're feeling stretched you are not on your own – a McKinsey study of 1,500 executives found that only nine per cent of the respondents were 'very satisfied' with their current time allocation and less than half 'somewhat satisfied'.

So how do we carve out time to work on new initiatives? We covered a piece of this in the stakeholder management section where we need to proactively manage, prioritise and use different communication strategies with various stakeholder groups. We need to do the same in allocating our time between the day-to-day business and working on key initiatives that will pave the way for more ongoing success. We also need to have time in between to meet with customers, manage and develop our team members, interface with key stakeholders, conduct deep-dives and so on.

When I was a sales leader, I tried to manage my day-to-day business with six to eight hours a week of key meetings. I found that a well-designed management system and reports along with efficient meeting practices could keep me across what was going on. That included forecast reviews with sales teams, reviews with all the other key functions in the business, and keeping track of metrics. If there was an area or two that needed additional attention we could set up a separate discussion and deep-dive into that topic. With six to eight hours blocked in the calendar every week to keep on top of business, there are still thirty-two to thirty-four hours left in a forty-hour week. Now, to lead a couple of key initiatives properly might take two to four hours of dedicated time per week, so let's block that out next. That still leaves around thirty hours to spend in the field with customers, work with our team members and do whatever else needs to get done in a week.

However, a lot of sales leaders, particularly in larger companies, are consumed with the day-to-day work, making it crucial to find a way to stay on top of things but get out of that busy loop so we have the time and capacity to work on new initiatives.

It's very easy for sales leaders to acknowledge the need for change, but it's so easy for everyone to go back to their old habits. There's no denying that when we try to do things differently, or introduce a new initiative, we're likely to run into hurdles, like navigating new systems, transitioning from existing processes, inertia from ingrained habits, dealing with other functions of the business and external parties – the list goes on. It's so important that when team members run into these barriers that you are there to help them through that or find a solution; this is where new initiatives can make it or break it.

Managers and team members are very busy already, so loading on a mandate to drive a change or new initiative isn't as easy as giving an instruction or getting a commitment to make it happen. As leaders, we need to be personally involved in every new initiative – at least up until a certain point.

Beyond that, how should we prioritise our time?

Colour your world

The first step is to assess how you're already spending your time. Tim Dwyer, managing director of Shirlaws Australia and creator of Growth Metrics Australia, has developed a simple colour-coding method to help leaders better manage their time.

Leaders simply colour-code all of the tasks in their calendar, based on the following guidelines:

- **Black: Strategy and future-focused tasks**. These are tasks that won't deliver revenue today, but will in the future.

- **Blue: Tasks that make money today**. This includes the activities of sales, marketing and customer service, as well as building products, delivery and team management.

- **Red: Tasks required to keep the business running**. This includes administration, HR, IT support, accounting and other background tasks. These tasks keep the business running, but don't directly contribute to revenue. On an individual level, email is a big one, along with some meetings.

I encourage you to colour-code your own calendar, and see which colours are most dominant. For example, are you spending most of your time on red and blue tasks? If so, this indicates you need to delegate some of those tasks to others, or find ways to manage them more effectively.

Delegating tasks

Many leaders are hesitant to delegate tasks. In fact, according to an executive coaching survey led by Stanford University, thirty-five per cent of chief executives say delegating is something they need to improve, yet only thirty-seven per cent are actively trying to improve these skills.

As leaders, why do we struggle to delegate? Possibly the biggest and most common difficulty with delegation revolves around accountability. When we delegate a task, we give up the responsibility for its execution, but we're still ultimately accountable for its success or failure. It can be difficult to trust others to complete tasks successfully and to a high standard. This is why it's so important to build trust over time, as discussed in Step 6.

Delegating also takes time and mentoring. If we delegate a task to someone and expect them to do as good a job as we would've done, we must take the time to outline the task in detail, including the objectives and goals, and give that person the necessary knowledge to complete the task successfully.

Despite the challenges of delegation, there are many advantages. By delegating, we create learning opportunities for our teams, as taking on new tasks helps team members develop and enhance their skills. This then leads to increased motivation and job satisfaction, which can then lead to increased loyalty among staff. Also, by delegating tasks, we reduce or eliminate potential bottlenecks, as our teams aren't waiting for us to make decisions or take action.

So, I say we should delegate at least one or two big tasks every year, because things will just keep piling up on us as leaders, particularly as we pursue new initiatives. As leaders, we're constantly accumulating jobs, roles and initiatives. We have to prune those pretty aggressively if we ever want to work on anything new. Let's say we were personally involved in a couple of big initiatives last year. Now they're embedded in the business and running well. We need to withdraw ourselves from those, reduce our involvement or roll them into the day-to-day management system. There may be a responsibility or a function you are managing that eats at your time, but is now mature and can now be delegated, or two functions could be combined under one of your direct reports – this relieves you and also gives one of your team members a great opportunity. We need to always look for opportunities to shed activities so that we've got the capacity to fully pursue new initiatives.

An effective change management framework

Once we've set our objectives and have freed up the time to pursue them, the next step is following an effective change management framework.

The gold standard of change processes is Professor John Kotter's change model, which features eight steps. However, in the interest of efficiency and ease of implementation, I've consolidated the model into three overarching stages: development, alignment and execution.

It is so critical that we address each of these stages, otherwise there is a significant risk of your initiative going off the rails. We can all relate to the following scenarios, I am sure.

In one scenario, a client of mine shared that one of their senior business leaders had unveiled a new initiative in a series of town hall meetings at various offices around the country. The initiative made sense, there was a lot of initial noise and posters went up around the office. But afterwards, nothing much happened and the initiative faded from sight, only to be replaced by more pressing priorities. While the concept for the initiative had been developed, there wasn't a focus on alignment or execution.

Meanwhile, another client wanted their sales team to focus on selling more complex solutions, rather than higher volume commodity products, and therefore deliver better margin outcomes. But the initiative just wasn't getting off the ground. These complex solutions took a longer time to sell since the sales process, the testing required and the due diligence for this type of purchase were more complex. When I dug into the situation, I found that the sales management was still focused on short-term targets. I also found that these deals required technical resources that were running at full capacity already. So management had launched a top-down initiative, but had not actually changed anything to support the execution of it. They had definitely not carved out time specifically to drive this initiative and iron out the wrinkles. Once they made some changes in their management system and dedicated time each week to reviewing progress and understanding the barriers to success, they started to get some great results.

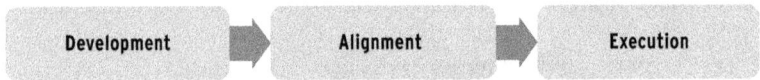

| Development | | Alignment | | Execution |

Figure 34: Change management framework

Development

This stage is about developing the initiative and solution. The first step is understanding the need for change and how we can create some urgency around it. Here are some questions to consider:

- What are the problems with the status quo?
- What are the implications for the business to continue in the same way?
- What is the business case for change?

Once we understand the need for change, and have everyone convinced that this is a must do, we will enlist a core team of change agents from relevant functions to help evaluate options and design the solution.

Involving stakeholders from different functions helps us not only develop a better solution, but also helps us get the buy-in we will need to make the initiative work. At different stages of the solution development, these change agents should check in and share progress with their respective functions to ensure the proposals will be effective and to bring back valuable feedback on how to improve the plan. The development stage is one of constantly testing and evaluating the viability of the initiative.

At the end of the development stage we should have a fully formed plan that has had input from all key stakeholders. We should then have confidence to enlist the broader organisation to get on board.

Alignment

The next step is to motivate and communicate. We should build a communication plan to share our initiatives with the relevant stakeholders, and pre-wire key management and opinion leaders with one-on-one advance briefings. This plan should be as wide as is relevant to the size of the initiative and the people affected. I've always found that you can never over-communicate your key priorities – it demonstrates your commitment to the initiative and the folks in support functions like to know what the sales priorities are so they can work out how they can best support them.

Again we want to present a strong case for change by demonstrating the benefits of making the change and the costs of maintaining the status quo. In doing so, we create a sense of urgency for the business to take action. A communication plan also ensures everyone understands how the change will affect them and their role, and how they can contribute. This creates additional motivation for the change, as employees have a sense of buy-in.

Execution

If we fail to execute the change properly, then it will eventually amount to nothing, meaning nothing will really change. In this final step, we need to create targets, both short term and long term, so that we can take appropriate action and boost the chances of success.

If you're in a mid- or large-size operation, consider *not* launching the initiative across the whole group, but instead starting with one team or one market segment. Focus on achieving success there, ironing out the kinks and achieving some quick wins, before launching more broadly.

It's also important to maintain ongoing communication and urgency about the change. We can do this by:

- Prioritising these discussions in management meetings
- Having meetings each week to track the progress of the change – not just end results, but digging into barriers, issues, resistance, unintended consequences, system problems and so on
- Staying visible and involved in the change by continuing to communicate its progress with our own teams

We should also consolidate gains so that we can achieve even more change. We can do this by celebrating early wins and breakthroughs, course correcting and improving initiatives as needed, and prioritising every change until it's embedded in the business.

Note that all three of these steps are critical to change success, and missing any key step is going to handicap your chances of making the initiative successful.

SUMMARY

That brings us to the end of the seven-step process for creating a future-proof, next-gen sales team. Before I share my final thoughts with you, here's a list of the key points from this chapter to remember:

- If we want our teams to survive and thrive, we must be proactive about internal change, which means constantly looking for ways to improve in order to get better results.

- Less than one third of launched initiatives are successful. Most initiatives are neither planned properly nor followed through by the leader.

- We must clearly prioritise which initiatives we will pursue. In order to determine which opportunities to pursue, and which ones to put on ice or bypass completely, we can use the opportunity matrix or a similar method that will give us a view on the relative difficulty and the rewards for each initiative.

- A lot of sales leaders, particularly in larger companies, are consumed with the day-to-day running of their business. We've got to find a way to get out of that loop, so we have the time and capacity to work on new initiatives. First step is to streamline your day-to-day management system and then allocate time for new initiatives.

- As leaders, we're constantly accumulating jobs, roles and initiatives. We have to prune those pretty aggressively if we ever want to work on anything new. Every year, we should try to get one or two big things off our desk.

- To drive new initiatives and changes successfully we must have a structured approach, and Kotter's model is well worth studying. Also keep in mind the three key phases for successful change management: development, alignment and execution.

- Change is not a one-off exercise. We should have improvement initiatives running at all times and build a core organisational capability to constantly drive change.

Conclusion: Where to from Here?

'The most unprofitable item ever manufactured is an excuse.'

JOHN MASON

The B2B sales landscape is facing a time of immense change.

Buyers are savvier, with more access to information, more knowledge, and higher expectations than ever before. With the growing commoditisation of products and solutions, they also have more options than ever before, meaning that if they don't get the experience they want, if they are forced to engage with a salesperson before they need to, or if the price isn't right, they can easily go elsewhere.

At the same time, buyers are more focused than ever on managing risk and delivering ROI, which means purchasing decisions now need to be made by a committee of up to seventeen people. From a sales perspective, there is far more room for error, and far more gaps through which prospects can leak out of the sales funnel.

Fortunately, there is hope. There are tools and strategies that the proactive sales leader can use to build the right team and deploy them in a way that will generate results in the modern sales landscape. This is what we've covered in this book.

After reading these pages, you now know the ideal sales structure to address the new sales landscape where customers hold the power. You can organise your team in a way that directly facilitates the customer-driven sales model, and will ensure more customers move from awareness to advocacy. You know how to recruit and retain the right talent to fill this model, thereby accelerating your results.

And you know how to empower your team to execute in all three of the core sales functions – prospecting and lead generation, middle-of-the-funnel core sales, and customer success.

However, sales transformation isn't possible in a silo, and forward-thinking sales leaders know that they need to effectively collaborate across their organisations in order to drive results and effective change. This is why collaboration, stakeholder management and change management form the backbone of the sales strategy recommended in this book.

As you implement this advice, you will see your sales team transform, and your career grow as a result. The prospecting function will start generating more than enough pipeline to exceed sales targets and keep the core sales team motivated. The core sales team will increase conversion rates by better qualifying leads, and selling them with insights and stories. Even better is that the deals they get will not be ones where the customers hold all the aces and the vendor business struggles with low margins or even losses – they will be negotiated as a win-win for all parties involved.

Not only will new customer acquisition and close rates accelerate, but the retention and growth of your *existing* customers will climb, thereby delivering more ROI for the business as a whole.

Ultimately, your organisation, your sales teams and your career will all be *future proof*.

So what's next?

If you haven't already, the key is getting started. *Future Proof Sales Strategy* is a complete toolbox, with enough initiatives to keep you and your team busy and growing for years to come.

It is time to take action. Take initiative and be assertive with your company leadership. Don't leave it to the CMO and CXO to drive all change within your organisation (and take all the resources). Sales is where the rubber hits the road, and the sales function has more than enough insight to bring value to the C-suite by building out a world-class sales operation.

It is time to invest in sales – with strategy, time and resources. And as the sales leader, it's *your* responsibility to make the case for change.

Ensure you have the best people in your team, and that they are deployed effectively. Start generating results, and make your case to the C-suite for further investment and resources. Drive change for your customers, for your team, and for your organisation.

It's time to lead your team into the future.

About the Author

Steven Norman is a seasoned frontline sales leader and general manager, with over twenty-five years' experience in consumer, SMB and enterprise sales. Throughout his career, he has worked for leading technology companies such as Dell, Targus and NEC, as well as small tech companies and start-ups. Over his career he has been responsible for over US$4 billion in sales.

His experience spans everything, including front-line sales roles, sales management, senior sales and marketing leadership and general management, working both directly with customers as well as via distribution channels. He has worked extensively across the Asia Pacific region and has also held roles with global responsibilities.

He is the founder of Growth Acumen, where he works with sales and business leaders on implementing world-class sales best practices and developing their leadership. His clients range from large, multinational tech companies to fast-growing SaaS organisations, plus a range of other businesses looking to scale up their sales capability.

Keen to future proof your sales organisation?

Did you enjoy the book and want to implement some or all of the seven steps? We are here to support you through that transformation journey. We have helped many organisations, large and small, transform their sales teams and dramatically improve their sales outcomes.

Some of the services we offer:

Sales Audit and Gap Analysis

Do you need outside expertise to analyse your current sales structure and sales processes? We apply a structured process to identify opportunities and give you our recommendations on the best path forward.

Sales Planning Workshops

Steven regularly works with senior management and sales leadership teams to conduct intense workshops which will identify key sales development opportunities and align necessary stakeholders on a concrete plan.

Sales Training Programs

A range of customisable sales training programs across key sales disciplines. Courses are delivered interactively with hands-on role plays and ongoing reinforcement sessions.

Keynote Speaking

Have a leadership or sales kick-off meeting planned? Steven has a range of customisable keynotes around world-class sales strategy that are sure to stimulate your audience.

Please contact us at:

Email: snorman@growthacumen.com.au
LinkedIn: www.linkedin.com/in/growth-coach
Website: www.growthacumen.com.au

GRØWTH
ACUMEN
Accelerating Your Success

www.ingramcontent.com/pod-product-compliance
Lightning Source LLC
Chambersburg PA
CBHW060406220326
41598CB00023B/3038